Praise for
Seeds of Leadership

Will Lukang's practical book, *Seeds of Leadership*, breaks the leadership development process into small, accessible steps that will help anyone grow. His approach inspires you to move forward. Each "seed" is brief, but not simple. You can begin them easily, but their richness will cause you to think deeply as you grow. The seeds are supported by action steps, and when you begin even one of them, you will experience new ideas and gain new energy. Then, a bonus comes when you discover how each seed fits with all the others. As you dig deeper into the ideas and treasures in this book, your life will produce fruit from the first seed to the last. Spend even a little time with this book and grow your leadership!

—**Mike Henry Sr.**, Chief Instigator of Follower of One, author of the *Marketplace Mission Trip*, and coauthor of *The Character-Based Leader*

If you are a well-established leader or aspiring to be one, driving change is a critical skill. Will Lukang's insights provide a GPS to guide and enhance your reflections and actions along the way. *Seeds of Leadership* is a must-read for anyone wanting to improve their leadership and outcomes. Particularly helpful are the practical examples and actionable notions including leadership style, clarity of goals and vision, team dynamics, culture and succession planning. Will's skillful way of using reflective exercise allows the reader to think deeply about the seeds of leadership. It's one of those special books you will continue to reflect on long after you've finished reading it.

—**Bob Bayles**, Partner, Kairos Executive Programs

From working at his family's convenience store to serving as a corporate leader, Will Lukang shares the seeds of growing an effective leadership path and life. There are so many unspoken traits on the journey to growth as a leader, and the author beautifully illuminates even the most subtle of characteristics and the steps to move into action. *Seeds of Leadership* is a must-read for those eager to grow in their leadership walk!

—**Deb Ingino**, CEO, Strength Leader Development

Will Lukang's book, *Seeds of Leadership*, masterfully combines his extensive experience, well-honed insight, and commitment to helping others to enable each reader to find their own cohesive whole. The reflections at the end of each chapter are invaluable guides to turn learning into doing. The book is an excellent resource for anyone who wants to be more in tune with their own capabilities and more effective at marshaling them to achieve excellence and supporting others to find satisfaction in their work.

—**Paula Kiger**, editor and writer at Big Green Pen

Will Lukang's *Seeds of Leadership* beautifully captures the essence of a living legacy. Leadership isn't just about achieving personal success—it's about cultivating others to lead and thrive when you're no longer at the helm. Will's story of succession planning demonstrates the ultimate act of selflessness: empowering others to step into their potential. This book teaches that a true leader creates a living legacy by nurturing future leaders, ensuring that their impact continues long after they've moved on. It's an inspiring guide for anyone who wants their leadership to live on through the positive impact of others.

—**Sonia Di Maulo**, founder of Harvest Performance and award-winning author of *The Apple in the Orchard*

Will Lukang's book, titled *Seeds of Leadership,* offers a practical roadmap for aspiring leaders seeking to enhance their skills and impact. Through self-discovery, resilience and a commitment to developing others, Lukang's insights empower readers to cultivate the mindset and habits of effective leaders. As Lukang, a trusted expert in his field, says, "Integrity is not a one-day value, it is an everyday value," which means it is a process you can reinforce daily with courageous decisions based on self-awareness and honesty. I highly recommend this book to anyone looking to gain valuable guidance on overcoming weaknesses, fostering intentional personal growth, and unlocking their leadership potential.

—**Dane Deutsch**, teacher, coach, author, veteran and entrepreneur

SEEDS OF LEADERSHIP

NURTURING
THE LEADER
WITHIN

Other Books by the Author
The Character-Based Leader

SEEDS OF LEADERSHIP

Nurturing the Leader Within

WILL LUKANG

EMERALD LAKE
BOOKS
Sherman, Connecticut

Seeds of Leadership: Nurturing the Leader Within

Copyright © 2024 Will Lukang

Cover design © 2024 by Emerald Lake Books

All rights reserved. No part of this book may be used or reproduced by any means, graphic, electronic or mechanical, including photocopying, recording, taping or by any information storage retrieval system, without the written permission of the publisher except in the case of brief quotations embodied in critical articles and reviews.

Books published by Emerald Lake Books may be ordered from your favorite booksellers or by visiting emeraldlakebooks.com.

Library of Congress Cataloging-in-Publication Data

Names: Lukang, Will, 1967- author.

Title: Seeds of leadership : nurturing the leader within / Will Lukang.

Description: Sherman, Connecticut : Emerald Lake Books, [2024]

Identifiers: LCCN 2024030279 (print) | LCCN 2024030280 (ebook) | ISBN 9781945847837 (paperback) | ISBN 9781945847844 (epub)

Subjects: LCSH: Leadership.

Classification: LCC HD57.7 .L845 2024 (print) | LCC HD57.7 (ebook) | DDC 658.4/092--dc23/eng/20240808

LC record available at https://lccn.loc.gov/2024030279

LC ebook record available at https://lccn.loc.gov/2024030280

To my wife and daughters:
Writing this book wouldn't have been possible
without your inspiration and support.

Contents

Preface xv
Developing Yourself 1
Chapter 1. Knowing Yourself 3
   Seedling Reflections: Knowing Yourself 6
Chapter 2. Valuing Yourself 9
   Seedling Reflections: Valuing Yourself 12
Chapter 3. Developing Character 15
   Seedling Reflections: Developing Character 17
Chapter 4. Assessing Yourself 19
   Seedling Reflections: Assessing Yourself 21
Chapter 5. Setting Priorities 23
   Seedling Reflections: Setting Priorities 26
Chapter 6. Becoming an Active Learner 29
   Seedling Reflections: Becoming an Active Learner 32
Chapter 7. Improving Continuously 33
   Seedling Reflections: Improving Continuously 36
Chapter 8. Seizing the Moment 37
   Seedling Reflections: Seizing the Moment 39
Developing Others 41
Chapter 9. Being a Role Model 43
   Seedling Reflections: Being a Role Model 46
Chapter 10. Embracing Leadership Styles 49
   Seedling Reflections: Embracing Leadership Styles 52
Chapter 11. Leading with Influence 55
   Seedling Reflections: Leading with Influence 57
Chapter 12. Promoting Shared Purpose 61

    Seedling Reflections: Promoting Shared Purpose 64
Chapter 13. Challenging the Status Quo **67**
    Seedling Reflections: Challenging the Status Quo 69
Chapter 14. Nurturing Others **71**
    Seedling Reflections: Nurturing Others 74
Chapter 15. Maintaining Relevance **75**
    Seedling Reflections: Maintaining Relevance 77
Looking to the Future **79**
Chapter 16. Changing of the Guard **81**
    Seedling Reflections: Changing of the Guard 83
Chapter 17. Moving Forward after Setbacks **85**
    Seedling Reflections: Moving Forward after Setbacks 89
Chapter 18. Acknowledging Others **91**
    Seedling Reflections: Acknowledging Others 94
Chapter 19. Putting It All Together **97**
Author's Note 105
Acknowledgments 107
About the Author 109

Preface

Any journey begins with a first step—one that requires the courage to commit to a decision and strength and dedication to carry it through.

My leadership journey began in 1998, when I transitioned from an individual contributor into a management position. I decided to pursue this career path because I realized I was passionate about fostering the talents and skills of the people I worked with.

Once I became a team leader, I was determined to learn and understand what it took to be successful in that role. I read voraciously and learned from other leaders—I was especially drawn to the philosophies of author and speaker John C. Maxwell.

In 2006, while working for a financial company and overseeing multiple teams, I decided to enroll in the Masters of Strategic Communication and Leadership program at Seton Hall University. The decision to pursue advanced studies was incredibly rewarding and gave me the tools necessary for success.

In my quest to gain leadership skills, I realized that mastering them required not only knowledge, but also daily practice. It was like planting and tending a seed: my emerging abilities required constant nurturing and attention.

It was one thing to be aware of what I needed to accomplish, but quite another to be consistent about the task. As I worked on developing each essential attribute of a strong leader, I envisioned the technique of planting a seed and growing a healthy seedling. Planting the seed meant investing the time to learn. Watering meant daily diligence and consistency. Nurturing the seedling meant reflecting, correcting and adjusting until I had mastered the skill in question and it became second nature.

For you to be an effective leader, you must have a solid base of knowledge and be open to new concepts. I love learning and continually seek out novel ideas and philosophies. Books have been an invaluable resource for me in this respect, and that is why I have developed this guide for leaders who want to strategically improve themselves and lead their organizations more efficiently.

But there are many books on becoming a leader. Why bother to read this one? Many leadership books focus simply on the qualities and characteristics of a leader and tell you that you need to develop them. This book provides some guidance and methods for how to actually do that.

You will see that the chapters are loosely collected into three primary topics: developing yourself, developing others, and planning for the future. If you've ever worked with me or heard me speak, these are what I refer to as the three "pillars of leadership."

The first pillar is self-leadership. Knowing yourself and understanding what you need to work on is crucial to being an effective leader.

The second pillar is leading others. As leaders, we help our organization by cultivating more leaders who can contribute significantly to its success.

The last pillar is planning for the future. Leaders must plan for their succession to ensure the organization can sustain its performance. By challenging our leaders to step up and take on more diverse roles, we can ensure that the organization's legacy remains strong.

When we master these three pillars of leadership—self-leadership, leading others, and planning for the future—we can build a resilient and thriving organization.

Within the framework of those three pillars, we'll explore how to identify qualities within yourself and others that are worth investing time and energy into, why it's important to value yourself even when no one else does, setting priorities for your self-improvement plan, critical elements to pay attention to when nurturing and mentoring others, creating a common vision and shared purpose, being prepared for the unexpected, and many other topics.

Each chapter concludes with a series of questions for you to ponder and answer through journaling. These can be found as "Seedling Reflections" at the end of each chapter. I suggest obtaining a sturdy notebook for this activity and using it exclusively for the writing you do in response to the prompts. A dedicated journal will allow you to go back and review your responses later and track your progress over time. (Since this practice is one you may want to apply periodically, I have prepared a PDF for you to download. It contains the "Seedling Reflections" questions from each chapter. You can request a copy by visiting emeraldlakebooks.com/SLpdf.)

One characteristic that marks a strong leader is their commitment to self-improvement and adding value to the lives of those with whom they work. By meeting your personal development goals, you will be a more effective mentor for others who want to develop their technical and leadership skills. To lead is to serve, and to serve is to ensure others become better by association.

DEVELOPING OURSELVES

CHAPTER 1

Knowing Yourself

Understanding oneself is crucial
for effectively helping others.

As the middle child in a Chinese family, I learned at a young age that there was a correlation between the success of my academic achievements and my parents' affection. My father and mother, Kim and Olympia, owned a convenience store in Pasay City, in the Philippines, and they encouraged education.

Both of my siblings did well in school, which made my parents happy. But I was different. I always had to work two or three times as hard for the same results and thus for my parents' goodwill. Sometimes I wondered what was wrong with me. I joked that when God bestowed the gift of intelligence on everyone, I'd only held out a small cup amid a crowd proffering large bowls.

Despite my academic efforts, my parents were extremely disappointed with my results and often told me I did not have a bright future. I began to believe I wasn't capable of success and started feeling sorry for myself. It was a vicious cycle: I worried so much about what my parents thought that my schoolwork suffered even more.

The one bright spot during my childhood, starting at the age of five, was working at my parents' convenience store after school. I enjoyed meeting and interacting with the customers, and I also learned valuable leadership lessons from my father. He put in an immense amount of hard work at the store because he wanted to lead by example. He was the first person there each day. My father never asked people to do work he wasn't willing to do himself. He stocked shelves, cleaned the floor in our warehouse, and carried supplies to and from the store, whether it was sunny or pouring rain.

He was humble, too. Even though he was the store owner, he usually dressed in a simple t-shirt and shorts. Sometimes when he pitched in to do hard physical labor, he would look really dirty too. But my father often counseled me to not judge people based on their appearance. He told me that what is inside is more important than what people see outside.

My father treated everyone the same, regardless of their social status and educational level, emphasizing the importance of respecting everyone and caring for one's employees. And he interacted with each customer with respect, asking them how they were doing instead of just going about his business. That's why, even today, I consciously greet employees who serve food or clean at hotels and restaurants. My father taught me that everyone is valuable and makes a difference.

Another bright spot appeared during my third year of high school when I met Araceli Ilao, a teacher who showed compassion for my situation and encouraged me as a student. It felt like someone was shining a light on my true potential. With her support, I began investing in myself.

I studied more and ignored the negativity I heard day in and day out, channeling my energy instead into proving everyone wrong. I still struggled, but I believed that as long as I had more good days than bad, I would keep moving forward. As part of the process, I made lists of my strengths and weaknesses, discovered my capabilities, and crafted plans to improve myself.

One goal that was very important to me was to focus on thinking positively about my situation and avoiding people who spoke negatively about me. I also began using affirmations. Each morning, I told myself, "You can do it. Never give up."

At first, I felt stupid because I still lacked self-confidence. A loud voice in my head echoed my parents' refrain: I had no future because of my lack of academic ability. But now, I consciously ignored that voice. Instead, I told myself I was ready to embrace the challenges that came my way and that I believed in myself.

After several months of doing this, I noticed a difference. My confidence grew and my grades improved. In my junior year of high school, I finished third in my class section. My teachers and parents noticed the change, and they were surprised and happy to see me make the honor roll. I was proud of my accomplishment and it motivated me to continue.

Each year, I learned more about myself and diligently chipped away at my list of weaknesses. And over time, that list got shorter and shorter.

In motivational speaker Wayne Dyer's book *Staying on the Path*, a collection of his quotations and observations, he wrote:

> With everything that has happened to you, you can either feel sorry for yourself or treat what has happened as a gift. Everything is either an opportunity to grow or an obstacle to keep you from growing. You get to choose.

Even though my childhood was difficult, I would not change anything because every experience helped form the foundation of my character and behavior. I accepted that I had challenges to overcome, planted the seeds of change, and maintained my willingness to learn and grow. I am grateful for the hardships I have faced, and I have come out stronger due to the paths I've chosen. Each scar I bear represents a valuable lesson learned and is a testament to my resilience and growth. My experiences have equipped me with insights and wisdom I will carry with me throughout my life and empowered me to support and uplift others on their own journeys.

> Plant the seed of patience. It takes time to recover from a setback or being at a disadvantage. But it is essential to learn your lessons and move on. Do not waver from your purpose. Be persistent. Make a list of your shortcomings and take time to really learn about yourself and develop a plan to change. It isn't easy, but turning your weaknesses into strengths charts your path to a successful life.

Seedling Reflections: Knowing Yourself

Answering these prompts in your journal will help you take your abstract ideas, decide on concrete goals, transform them into plans, and make real changes.

Personal strengths and growth

- Create a list of the specific strengths you have, such as being a problem solver, an active listener, or having a strong attention to detail.
- How do your strengths help you be a better leader?
- What specific actions can you take this week that make use of your strengths?

Weaknesses and improvement strategies

- Create a list of your weaknesses, such as procrastinating, being too quick to draw conclusions, or being impatient with employees. For each weakness, answer the following questions:
    - How can you improve?
    - When will you begin working on it? (Start now. Don't wait another day!)
    - How can you measure your progress, and how often will you do it?

Handling setbacks

- What will you do if you have a setback, find yourself at a disadvantage, or encounter resistance?
- Who can help you get back on track?
- What lessons can you learn?

Accountability and support

- Find someone to be an accountability partner. Share your plan with this person and check in regularly for six months to share and document your progress.

CHAPTER 2

Valuing Yourself

*If you don't see your own value,
others won't acknowledge it either.*

John C. Maxwell is my favorite author. I've learned a lot from him and appreciate this idea he shared in *The 15 Invaluable Laws of Growth*:

> If you put a small value on yourself, rest assured, the world will not raise the price.

As a child, I was so used to hearing I wasn't smart and wouldn't be able to accomplish anything that I was effectively programmed to accept this as reality. When you're consumed by the thought that you're not capable, you stop trying because you think your efforts will not yield any results.

I saw improvements in my academic work and career after I started putting in effort and stopped listening to negative voices. At last, there was hope. I began to recognize that if I didn't value myself, no one else would. To make progress, I needed to believe in myself and change my way of thinking. By adjusting my behavior and attitude about my daily challenges, I felt better about my future.

As Louise L. Hay wrote in *You Can Heal Your Life*:

> You have been criticizing yourself for years, and it hasn't worked. Try approving of yourself and see what happens.

I took this lesson to heart.

In my case, I slowly increased my overall confidence during the educational journey I described in the Preface. After high school, I was accepted into the University of Santo Tomas (UST), a top five institution in the Philippines, to study accounting. During my junior year, I was appointed external vice president for the UST chapter of the Junior Philippine Institute of Accountants. To be an officer, you must be a class representative in your junior year of college and serve the organization.

As the external vice president, I was tasked with representing our university. I was not comfortable in my new role, particularly when speaking in public and interacting with folks from other top-tier universities, but I nevertheless constantly pushed and challenged myself and reflected on the progress I'd made so far.

Although I successfully graduated with a degree in accounting, I decided not to tackle the board exam. I wanted to pursue programming for my career instead. However, one of my professors insinuated that the real reason I wasn't taking the exam was because I had not learned the material well enough. Her comments took me aback, and I decided to prove her wrong. But as I reviewed the test prep materials in the six months leading up to the board exam, self-doubt set in and I was beset with worries, especially since I hadn't passed any of the practice tests, which increased my anxiety. My mother also expressed concern about my ability to succeed. I kept studying, though, determined to persevere.

As nervous as I was, the four-day board exam was a grueling exercise covering eight topics. Traditionally, only 18 percent of those who take it pass. But I did so on my first try. I was so proud of myself! I had proved that I am capable, and I learned that failure is a step toward success—it's a learning experience.

Yet, despite my success with the board exam, I immediately suffered another setback. The very next morning, my father woke me up at 3:30 a.m. and handed me the key to our convenience store. He wanted me to take over. I was shocked and told him I had other career plans. I had two job offers I was considering: one at a top accounting firm and another as a programmer for a financial company. But now, my dreams went up in smoke as my parents explained they had decided long ago that I would take over the store.

In traditional Chinese culture, children do not have decision-making authority—parents know best, and their guidance often extends to decisions made in adulthood. To disobey is unthinkable. So, with a heavy heart, I declined both job offers and went to work for my parents. I spent the next two years managing the store.

During that time, when I got together with friends and they talked about their careers and promotions, it was difficult. Our conversations constantly reminded me that my peers were moving ahead with their lives while I was standing still. When it was my turn to share updates about my life, they would say, "Oh yes! You're watching your family's convenience store." It seemed like my years of struggle and effort meant nothing. I had ended up at my parents' store anyway. My future seemed dim, which was extremely disappointing for me. After six months, I stopped getting together with my friends because I felt stuck and had nothing new to share.

For the next two years, I went to a job each day that I was not passionate about doing. It didn't fulfill me, and I didn't really enjoy it. Finally, I mustered up the courage to tell my mother I didn't want to work at our store. I offered to leave her house if that was what it took to move on. In traditional Chinese families, children stay with their parents until they get married, unlike in Western culture, where they move out after high school. My declaration of independence shocked her.

Surprisingly, my sister immediately announced that she would take over the store as soon as she graduated, which was a few months down the road. That satisfied my parents and allowed me to move on. In retrospect, I am grateful I had the courage to speak up. If I hadn't, I would still be working at that store!

Sometimes, learning to stand up for yourself can help you achieve a different outcome. It was easier for me to overcome these obstacles and the negativity I faced because I had consciously recognized my worth and accomplishments. That helped me develop my confidence and make progress.

> Plant the seed of valuing yourself. Facing setbacks or negativity from people we love or look up to can trick us into believing that we are not capable. Reminding ourselves of the successes we've already had and ignoring naysayers strengthens our sense of self-worth. Focus on achieving specific incremental goals to improve your confidence. Each success will help you move forward and will bolster your belief that you can change your life.

Seedling Reflections: Valuing Yourself

Sometimes we don't recognize our own value or worth until we sit down and analyze our character. In this exercise, take the time to identify those qualities in yourself.

Identifying unique attributes

- List the attributes that make you special—such as kindness, generosity, cheerfulness—or any other quality that stands out. If this exercise is challenging, find someone whose opinion you trust and ask them to help you identify your positive traits.
- What qualities do your friends, family and colleagues frequently commend you for?

Reflecting on positive experiences

- Write about an experience where you used each of the attributes you've identified.
- Did that experience make you feel good about yourself? If so, how? If not, why not?

Chapter 2. Valuing Yourself

Daily affirmations

- Start each day by either writing or vocalizing this affirmation: "I will do my best and seize the moment." Use this statement to develop your confidence and remind yourself that you have the ability to work through challenges.

- Create a personal mantra that resonates with your leadership goals and repeat it throughout the day to reinforce your positive mindset. What is it, and why did you choose it?

Acknowledging positive influences

- Identify a person who has touched your life in a positive way or helped you overcome a specific difficulty. How did that person encourage you? How did you change as a result?

- When you feel discouraged, reread what you wrote in your journal to remind yourself that you have overcome challenges before and you are perfectly able to do so again.

CHAPTER 3

Developing Character

Character forms the bedrock of
our reputation.

Becoming a good leader begins with being a good person. Your values and beliefs help guide your company. I vividly remember a lesson I learned from Professor Karl Soehnlein at Seton Hall. He defined leadership as the relationship between leaders and those they serve, a relationship that is only possible if people trust you. At that moment, I decided integrity would be the cornerstone of my behavior going forward.

Your character, which includes your values, integrity and behavior, is the foundation upon which your reputation is built. Essentially, the way you act (especially when no one is watching) and the principles you uphold shape how others perceive you. A strong, positive character leads to a good reputation, while a weak or negative character results in a poor one.

As I have climbed the proverbial corporate ladder, I've always kept in mind that my character is more important than any accomplishment I might achieve in my lifetime. I try to ensure that I do the right thing, no matter what the situation is. I also conduct myself based on the values I believe in.

This has not always been easy. For example, one time, when I was building a team to focus on quality assurance engineering, I hired two individuals who were both strong employees in their respective domains. But about a year into their tenures, each one received a lucrative offer to work for another firm. I was sad to see them go because I was unable to match what the other companies were offering. However, a few months after their departure, they both reached out to me independently and asked about returning to our team.

I could have ignored them because they had left us and it had taken quite a bit of time and effort to find new people to replace them. But I chose to do the right thing. Our company happened to have open roles, and I offered them positions. They both ended up working for us again.

It is easy to fall into the trap of holding grudges, and I could have ignored their requests to return. But I stayed aligned with my values—doing what was best for my team and the company—and brought them back.

Merriam-Webster defines integrity as a "firm adherence to a code of especially moral or artistic values." How much we prize integrity often depends on the values our parents instilled in us. Be grateful if this is a lesson your elders stressed. Otherwise, recognize that while your upbringing shaped you, it does not define you. Although we can be shown and taught the values we need, it's up to you to mold your own character. You have the gift of choice. Acknowledge your flaws and work to correct them. It is never too late. Change now and be better tomorrow. Here's how to begin:

1. **Surround yourself with good people.** Associate with individuals who will keep you honest. Create an environment where colleagues can tell you the truth, not simply agree with you to flatter or gain favor.

2. **Value your family.** Your family helps define you. Those closest to you shape your values, beliefs and foundation. At work, reflect the values you prize in your family life.

3. **Connect with a source of inspiration.** Pray, meditate or spend time in nature to remind yourself that you are part of something bigger. Allow this more holistic vision of the world to shape your journey and help you grow and develop.

4. **Don't compromise your values.** Be firm about what you will and won't do. There will always be gray areas, but don't cross your ethical boundaries.

5. **Do the right thing.** Make choices that are in line with your values. When you are faced with a difficulty at work, address it in a way you can be proud of.

6. **Take time to reflect.** Step back consistently to evaluate your decisions and practices. Make sure you are being true to yourself.

Integrity is not something you use only when it's convenient; it is an everyday value. And using it is a process. You cannot check a box labeled "integrity" and move on. You can't buy it, and it can't be bestowed upon you. Integrity is a value that you reinforce daily by making the correct choices and decisions. Remember, integrity is the foundation of strong leadership. If that foundation is weak, the organization will crumble.

> Plant the seed of self-awareness and honesty in yourself and nurture it. Continually audit your conduct and align your choices with your beliefs. As the American college basketball coach John Wooden says:
>
> > Be more concerned with your character than your reputation, because your character is what you really are, while your reputation is merely what others think you are.
>
> Focus on developing and improving your character and everything else will fall into place.

Seedling Reflections: Developing Character

These questions are designed to help you reflect on the importance of character in leadership. Consider your values and beliefs and write down your thoughts. After answering the questions, consider sharing your insights with your accountability partner.

Personal character assessment

- In your own words, define what "character" means to you.
- Reflect on how your upbringing has influenced your understanding of character.
- Identify times when you have demonstrated strong character in your leadership roles or personal life.

Character practices and strategies

- Reflect on the importance of surrounding yourself with trustworthy individuals in a leadership role.
- How do your family values align with your leadership values?
- Identify a moment when you had to make a difficult decision that tested your character. How did you handle it, and what did you learn?

Integrity development plan

- Write about how you maintain your character in challenging situations. Are you satisfied with how you do it?
- Consider some ways to integrate a sense of connection to the wider world or personal inspiration into your leadership journey.
- Think about the concept of doing the right thing, even when no one is watching, and the impact that has on leadership character.

Reflection exercise

- Decide on a process for regularly reflecting on your decisions and practices to ensure your actions are in alignment with your values. What will it be, and when will you do it?
- Think of a specific example of how you have strengthened your character as a leader over time. When was it, and what did you learn?

CHAPTER 4

Assessing Yourself

Self-assessment acts like a mirror, reflecting areas that need improvement and guiding you toward becoming a better leader.

Good leaders understand that self-improvement is an ongoing process. For some, it can be quite painful. It requires evaluating yourself honestly and facing your weaknesses. It also requires you to assess your strengths and the possibilities that lie before you. I like to use an exercise I came up with that I call "Strengths, Weaknesses, Opportunities and Interests" to determine where I stand on my leadership journey.

Each year, I make a point of doing an assessment of my performance. I compare my last plan for what I wanted to achieve with what I accomplished and then focus on identifying improvement. The purpose of this exercise is not to compare myself to others, but to compare myself to where I was at previously.

Assessment is a crucial aspect of leadership development. Without proper evaluation, we cannot identify the areas where it's necessary to improve so we can achieve our personal and organizational goals. This exercise allows me to celebrate successes and create a plan for areas that need improvement.

As you complete your own assessment, know that your strengths are the keys to your success. Focus on those abilities and continue to showcase them. The areas where you shine balance out the areas where you struggle.

1. Make a list of your strengths—the things that make you unique and most able to contribute.

2. For each one, consider how you can amplify it. Write down actionable steps to leverage and enhance your strengths further.

Next, take a look at the areas where you can improve. As Sigmund Freud said, "Being entirely honest with oneself is a good exercise." Still, it might be daunting for you if you are your own worst critic, because facing your weaknesses can leave you feeling vulnerable. But a self-assessment isn't intended to create a crisis of self-doubt. In fact, its goal is exactly the opposite. You want to understand where you need to improve so you can grow. This understanding is crucial to success.

1. List your three biggest weaknesses.

2. Identify specific steps you can take to overcome these weaknesses.

3. Establish milestones and set dates by which you will have achieved them.

4. Create a list of individuals who can assist you in your endeavors. Consider seeking guidance from mentors and coaches who can provide support and assistance in your journey of personal and professional development.

In the next part of this process, you must seek opportunities to understand the unknown. They rarely come to us gift-wrapped with a bow. We must seek them out and be ready to make a move when the chance comes along.

Finally, it is critical to understand your true interests and motivations and how those relate to your goals. You are much more likely to be successful in a field where your skills and interests align.

- What are you passionate about? What do you love to do?

- If you could have your dream job, what would it be?

- How close is your current position to your dream job?
- How are you measuring your progress?
- What areas of interest have you not yet explored?

Look back at your list of interests. What steps could lead you to the job you've always longed to have? Will you be prepared when the opportunity arises?

To gain clarity about what you need to work on, ask yourself these questions:

- What am I doing that is effective and needs to continue?
- What am I not doing that I need to start doing?
- What am I doing that is not effective and needs to stop?

> Plant the seed of self-assessment. Be aware of how you stack up against others in your industry. Understanding your strengths helps you further develop them, while understanding your weaknesses helps you improve and grow. By seeking opportunities to uncover your blind spots and further improve your abilities as a leader and by delving deeper into your interests, you will continuously enhance your skills and effectiveness.

Seedling Reflections: Assessing Yourself

These prompts invite you to consider how a good leader handles themselves and how closely aligned you are with that model. Write your answers in your journal.

Reflecting on leadership challenges

- Describe a situation where you took on a leadership role and it went poorly. How might you have improved the way you handled it?
- If you were to ask your team how effective you are as a leader, what would they say?

- Write about a time where you asked for feedback. If you don't do this, why not?

Decision-making and ethics

- Write about a situation where you made a tough decision. Describe the scenario and the outcome. As you reflect on it, how might you have handled things differently?
- What does it mean to you to "do the right thing" at all times?
- If you had a choice between being good and being right, which would you choose and why?

Nurturing your team

- Describe a situation in which you allowed your team to make an important decision. What was the outcome?
- Describe the culture of your team. What are the team's dynamics?
- Do you promote psychological safety, and do your team members feel comfortable voicing their concerns and sharing their ideas?
- Identify a specific situation where a team member did approach you with a concern or idea. What specifically did you do that made that person believe they could come to you?

CHAPTER 5

Setting Priorities

Keep your major priorities front and center
before tackling other tasks.

When I was fourteen years old, my father and a group of store owners formed a volunteer fire brigade to protect their block of convenience stores in the Pasay Market. By contributing their own money and collecting donations, they were able to purchase an old fire truck. I was too young to be a firefighter, but because of my first aid training from the Boy Scouts, I was asked to serve as the medic. It was my first experience of helping others, and I loved it.

At that point, my dream was to don fireman's gear and join the brigade. Thanks to a growth spurt, I was finally able to when I turned fifteen. No matter how hard the day was, I came home with a smile. Our work was important: we were saving lives and people's homes. Over the next nine years, my life revolved around this service, and I was eventually promoted to assistant commander.

Serving others is still important to me, and I often step out of my comfort zone to do so. But at times, I've overextended myself with commitments to others at the expense of my own obligations. This made me feel overwhelmed and stressed, so I decided to make a change. I drew up a list of what mattered most to me and chose to consistently address the items at the top of the list first. I've found that when I stick to this plan, my life feels balanced and on track.

We all have the tug and pull of competing priorities: work, family, social commitments and hobbies. And to become good leaders, we will need to take on additional responsibilities at work, diving into new classes or coursework to learn a new skill, and agreeing to mentor new hires at work. Each task we need to take care of will compete with other tasks, or we will end up jumping from one thing to another, getting confused about what to focus on next and never accomplishing anything.

If we don't determine what's important to us, we may not have enough time to spend on the goals that matter most. In his book *First Things First*, Stephen R. Covey, probably best known as the author of *The 7 Habits of Highly Effective People*, categorizes priorities as "big rocks" and less important tasks as sand, pebbles or small rocks. In his metaphor, he explains that when filling a jar (in other words, when allocating our time), it is essential to put the big rocks in first; otherwise, the smaller objects will fill up all the available space and the big rocks—the really important ones—will not fit.

My big rocks are family, health, work and serving others. But if you ask a group of five people to name their most important goals, you may get five different answers because every individual's goals and values vary. However, determining what you value is essential to accomplishing what you desire in life. To help you do this, consider these questions:

- Which people and activities are important to you?

- What is your dream in life? What do you seek to achieve?

- What is your life purpose? Is it providing for your family, volunteering for a favorite charity, or helping others?

- What lasting impression do you want to leave in this world? Are you a giver or a taker?

Identifying your priorities may seem like a simple process, but it really isn't. Our priorities change as our lives do. It is important to step back regularly, refocus and ask yourself the questions above to see if your values have shifted.

Chapter 5. Setting Priorities

Once you've identified your priorities, you can focus your energy on tasks related to your goals. If you feel you have wasted a lot of time on pebbles, don't worry! It's never too late. You can start changing things today by making a list of your big rocks and reprioritizing those.

Another critical aspect of prioritization is managing your energy. In his book *Energize*, life coach Simon Alexander Ong states that your energy is the fuel that drives your success and gives you the power to achieve your potential. Before reading this book, I'd never thought about managing my energy expenditures, even though I was jumping from task to task, trying to accomplish too many things, and my health was suffering! Since I didn't prioritize my needs, I found myself facing high blood pressure, prediabetes and weight gain.

After reading Ong's book, I learned to design my day around the times when I have the most energy and devote those times to accomplishing the more important things. You might assume you have the most energy in the morning; but it varies from person to person. You need to assess when you have the most energy and maximize your opportunities. As Ong puts it, "You can do amazing things, but only if you have the energy to do them."

As I conclude this chapter, a quote often attributed to H. L. Hunt comes to mind.

> Decide what you want, decide what you are willing to exchange for it. Establish your priorities and go to work.

Once you have established what is most valuable to you, deciding to let go of small things and focusing on what is most important becomes easier. When we understand what really matters to us, we make better choices.

> Plant the seed of prioritizing and align your activities with what you hope to achieve in life. There are many demands on your time and attention, so to live a meaningful life, you must understand your purpose and prioritize.

Seedling Reflections: Setting Priorities

Don't skip this exercise—it is perhaps the most essential of them all! Understanding your values and setting priorities will help you see the big picture and move toward your dream more efficiently.

Identifying your priorities

- Without overanalyzing, make a list of all your current obligations.

- Review your list of obligations and number them in order of importance. Are there any you want to focus on? Or others that, after some thought, you want to eliminate from your list?

Daring to dream

- What are your biggest goals and ambitions? Write them down. What would have to happen for you to know you've accomplished what you set out to do?

- Describe how you will feel when you achieve your goals.

- Make a list of the tasks standing between you and your dream.

- Set a due date for each task and create a timeline for completing them.

Building success habits

- Each day, take a moment to visualize your dream, then look at your task list and choose one item to work on that will bring you closer to your goal. What will it be, and how will it bring you closer to your goal?

- Compare your list of priorities with your to-do list. Make sure you are addressing the most important items first. Are there any things that can be removed from the list?

- Be careful of accepting responsibilities that don't correspond to your priorities. Are there any tasks on your list that someone else should be responsible for? If so, what are they, and how will you ensure they are reassigned to the right person?

- And really… Start today. Don't procrastinate! What's one step that you'll take today to start building your success habits?

CHAPTER 6

Becoming an Active Learner

Leaders are always learning.

Good leaders are not born; they are created through a combination of learned skills and experience on the job. I like to compare the journey of becoming a successful leader to a pyramid. The base requires a wide breadth of knowledge, followed by an understanding of how that knowledge applies within a business context. The next layer is the ability to focus and apply that knowledge and understanding specifically to the workplace. When these three things come together, good leadership becomes possible.

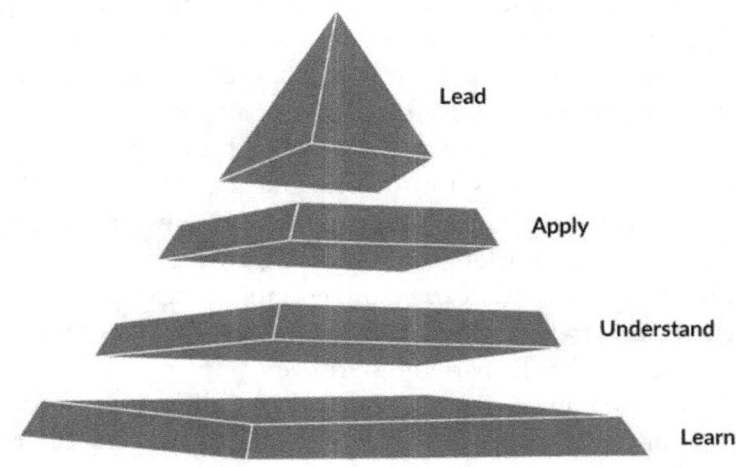

You can build your knowledge by reading books and articles, taking leadership training courses, and finding a mentor or coach. For example, I joined the John Maxwell Team program, a leadership certification program, to develop my skills. (The name has changed since then to the Maxwell Leadership Certified Team.)

Another method is to identify leaders you admire. Which qualities do they have that you wish to emulate?

It is also important to create a yearly growth plan to guide your own improvement. This blueprint will help you achieve your goals by guiding your activities and decisions.

My growth plan has the following categories:

- **A list of books I want to read:** Once I've completed a book, I will write five takeaways from it that I want to remember.

- **A list of training classes to complete:** This includes exploring new technologies or methodologies.

- **Above and beyond items:** In this section, I list my stretch goals. For example, for 2024, I decided to host a virtual event on career breakthroughs.

Having a plan is essential because it allows you to track your progress throughout the year.

Actively seeking learning is an essential part of becoming a good leader, but all the knowledge in the world is useless if you don't know how to apply it in context. For example, when my wife and I purchased our home, a friend gave us a new grill. I've assembled many grills, so I figured I knew enough to put this one together easily. The process was smooth, and after two hours, it was almost complete—except for one mystery part. I was perplexed; I had no idea where it belonged. My wife gently suggested I consult the instructions, where I learned this essential component must be added at the very beginning of the assembly. I had no choice but to take the entire grill apart and start over.

I'd assumed my knowledge and understanding were thorough enough for me to assemble the grill, but when the time came to apply what I knew, I needed to go back and gather more information to complete the task successfully. In the workplace, textbook knowledge may not apply neatly to every situation. Sometimes you have to return to the drawing board to find an appropriate solution.

There is no direct, linear path to becoming a good leader. Reading books or attending a conference won't suddenly transform you into an effective manager. Like the transformation from baby to child or teenager to adult, each step in the leadership process requires time. Similarly, fledgling leaders must decide how they will behave and conduct themselves, learning from past mistakes and determining the best way forward. Leaders who have the humility to recognize and acknowledge their mistakes and learn from them have a bright future.

A good leader must also find ways to encourage and inspire others while simultaneously meeting deadlines and client demands. As a leader progresses through the different levels of responsibility and management, they become more experienced and their competence grows. Years of gaining knowledge, combined with real-life experience, allow a person to guide others well.

With a business environment as fluid and changeable as ours is today, managers must also constantly evaluate how their operations measure up. Some fundamental questions are: What will our leadership look like in five years? Will our people be prepared for new roles and challenges? Which changes and training will elevate us to the next level?

Leaders need to be open to new ideas so they can guide their organizations forward as time and technology change. Think of it as natural selection—only the fittest will survive.

Finally, to guide a company successfully, the leader must have their team's best interests at heart. The greater good must eclipse self-promotion. This is the next level of learning, and it is only possible after you've been in a leadership position for some time. At that point, you will be developing leaders around you by mentoring, coaching and training, which in turn means the organization increases its capacity, propelling it to the next level.

> Plant the seed of learning. See yourself as a work in progress. Each day, seek to learn something new.

Seedling Reflections: Becoming an Active Learner

A good leader continues to grow so they can help others. Reflect on your learning process and record your answers in your journal to look back on later.

Learning

- Do you allocate time each year to learn something new? How do you identify and prioritize learning opportunities? How do you decide how much time to allocate to that task?

- Do you already have a strategy for personal growth and development? If so, write about your process. If not, outline the steps you will take to learn something this year.

Understanding and applying

- Write about a time where you learned something new and successfully applied it to benefit your team. How did it affect their performance?

- Think about whether you involve your team in analyzing key learnings. If you do, write about an example and the outcomes. If you don't, reflect on what prevents you from engaging in team exercises.

Leading others

- What do you admire in the leaders that you know? Write about your values and the kind of leader you want to be.

- How do you ensure you always lead with the best interests of your team or company in mind? Write about a situation where you prioritized the team's best interests.

- What is your strategy for developing leaders to prepare the team for future challenges and opportunities? If you don't currently have a strategy, write down your ideas for developing one.

CHAPTER 7

Improving Continuously

Leaders focus on continuous improvement
to empower their teams to achieve
exceptional results.

I often struggle with overcoming my weaknesses. One of the methods I've developed to help is a list of habits, practices or behavior that prevent me from making progress. I call this my "do-not-do list." For example, procrastinating has been number one on my list for many years. The do-not-do list helps you prioritize and eliminate behaviors that hold you back.

In 2008, when I graduated from Seton Hall University, I made a list of goals. One of them was writing a book of my own. As I thought about that goal, I laughed—I am not a particularly strong writer, and it seemed comical that I would even consider writing a book. However, I know I have a unique story to tell, and I am always willing to push myself out of my comfort zone, so I left this goal on my list. Though I had a desire to write, I never followed through with a specific commitment. Instead, I procrastinated year after year, full of good excuses about why I couldn't quite get to it. Finally, in 2014, I decided to get to work. This book is the result of my efforts. I have weaknesses just like anyone else, but I have an equal amount of determination to turn my areas of struggle into strengths.

I use this method for creating a do-not-do list, and I find it helpful for planning actionable goals that help me avoid certain behaviors:

1. Fold a piece of paper along the middle to create two columns. Label the column on the left "Weaknesses" and the column on the right "Action Items."

2. In the "Weaknesses" column, list any behavior or habit that interferes with your progress or growth.

3. In the "Action Items" column, outline specific actions you could take to eliminate or improve each weakness.

4. Make a note of the impact each weakness has on you: high, medium or low? How does each one hold you back? Rank them in order of how much negative impact they are having on your life.

5. Start working on the weakness that is holding you back the most. Review your list daily to remind yourself of which actions you want to incorporate into your schedule.

6. Create a goal sheet that lists your actions and use it to track your progress. You are much more likely to stick to the plan and assess yourself honestly if you keep a written record.

The do-not-do list is not static. Revisit it as often as possible. Perhaps you have overcome a bad habit or two and can add a new weakness to the list.

Remember, self-improvement is a critical component of growth and development; if you are not learning, you are falling behind. And don't forget to persevere! You will have highs and lows as you make these changes, but don't be discouraged and don't stop. Persistence and consistency are essential to success.

Although we often pay a lot of attention to our weaknesses, I believe we should pay equal attention to improving our strengths. By adopting this balanced approach, leaders can continue to excel in areas they are good at while making steady progress in areas where they may need improvement. Focusing solely on weaknesses can be draining and counterproductive in the long run.

Try making a "to-do" list, similar to the one above, but that focuses on good qualities that you'd like to improve upon, instead of weaknesses you'd like to eliminate or minimize.

1. Fold a piece of paper along the middle to create two columns. This time, label the column on the left as "Strengths." Keep the "Action Items" header for the column on the right.

2. In the "Strengths" column, list the behaviors or habits you are proud of and that are particularly useful to you in the workplace.

3. In the "Action Items" column, list specific things you can do to enhance or build on things you already do well. For example, if you're known for being a compassionate leader, perhaps do more reading on communication methods. Remember, teaching can often help cement our skills in a particular area, and mentoring is not only a way of enhancing your strengths, but also those of your team members.

4. Note how your strengths help you and whether they have a high, medium or low impact on your daily life and interactions with team members.

Plant the seed of continuous improvement to overcome your weaknesses and cultivate new strengths. By doing so, you are better prepared to support and assist your team effectively. In addition, commit to becoming a better version of yourself.

Seedling Reflections: Improving Continuously

Continuous improvement is vital for preparing yourself and your team to thrive both today and tomorrow. Use these prompts to set goals for yourself that contribute to ongoing growth and readiness.

Creating your Do-not-do list

- From your worksheet, choose three items you recognize as hindrances to your progress and performance. What are they, and how do they hold you back?
- Outline specific actions you want to take to prevent yourself from reverting to these old habits.

Creating your To-do list

- From your worksheet, choose three strengths you want to build on to become an even better leader. What are they, and why are they important to you?
- Outline the specific actions you want to take to enhance each strength.

Tracking your progress

- Create a goal sheet in your journal listing the actions you intend to take and use it to track your progress. You are much more likely to stick to the plan and assess yourself honestly if you keep a written record.

CHAPTER 8

Seizing the Moment

Embrace the present and seize every opportunity. Your actions today hold profound significance for tomorrow.

David Tolley is a highly regarded pianist and composer. He has written off-Broadway musicals and performed for four US presidents. In December 1985, however, he was just a regular person. Clad in a Nike T-shirt, faded jeans and flip-flops, he was attending a taping of *The Tonight Show* when host Johnny Carson asked if any audience members had played the piano for more than five years. Their guest pianist for the evening, Horatio Gutierrez, had had an accident and couldn't appear. Tolley raised his hand, and he was invited onstage. He played "Memory" from the Broadway hit *Cats* and it launched his career. He gave the best audition of his life in a situation where he had only planned to be a spectator.

Tolley's story reminds us to seize the opportunities that cross our path. With the right set of skills and a little courage, we can change the direction of our lives.

To give a personal example, I started my career as a mainframe developer, but when the internet became popular, I decided to become a web developer instead. I saved money and bought a Gateway computer for almost $3,000. I also bought books on HTML, JavaScript and CSS, then spent the next eight months practicing most weeknights until 2 or 3 a.m. Eventually, I mastered all three, as well as Microsoft's scripting language, ASP.

Two years later, I was consulting at Merrill Lynch and they needed a demo site for a web interface so users could access mainframe data. I told my manager I wanted the job and offered to complete it on my own time after work. He agreed to let me try. After a few weeks, I showed him my prototype, and he liked it. Because I'd done so well, they offered me a position on their web development team to see the project through. My preparations had allowed me to seize a new opportunity. This didn't happen by accident—I was ready when the opportunity presented itself.

I've always dedicated time to prepare for future opportunities within my growth plan, which serves as a guide to help me achieve my aspirations. By reviewing and checking off items regularly, I ensure I am continually progressing toward my goals. By doing this, I am following the wisdom of Confucius, who once said:

> Success depends upon previous preparation, and without such preparation there is sure to be failure.

My proactive approach has proven invaluable because I often find myself equipped with the necessary skills or training to seize opportunities as they arise. Being prepared enhances my chances of qualifying for them. I frequently emphasize to my mentees the importance of such preparation. By preparing yourself for what you hope to achieve, you make yourself future-ready and poised to capitalize on whatever comes your way.

To seize your own moment, you need to know what you want. Prepare yourself by asking:

- What do you want to achieve? What are you passionate about? What are your interests?

- What training do you need to achieve your goal? Do you need a new skill? If so, how can you acquire it?

- Who (which mentor or coach) can guide your journey? A coach can ask you tough questions and push you outside your comfort zone.

- How much time will you dedicate to your progress? Get started and be disciplined. Do not give up, and work on it every day.

> Plant the seed of preparation. Know your goal, work hard to hone your skills, and seize the chance when it crosses your path. Be intentional about maintaining your plan; that way, it is always up to date.

Seedling Reflections: Seizing the Moment

Staying in the present and seizing moments of opportunity are important to achieving success. Use these journal prompts to prepare yourself to take advantage of future opportunities.

Maintaining awareness

- What methods can you use to remind yourself to stay in the moment and maximize your interactions with other people?
- Reflect on a moment when you seized an opportunity. What led you to recognize and act on it?

Approaching new opportunities

- Describe your mindset when approaching new opportunities or challenges.
- How do you prepare yourself mentally and physically to take on these challenges when you're unsure how it will go?

Learning from challenges

- Think about a situation where you faced obstacles in seizing an opportunity. How did you overcome these challenges? What lessons did you learn?
- Which strategies do you use to stay resilient and persistent? Are there others you can add to your toolbox?

Sharing and inspiring others

- How do you inspire and encourage others to seize opportunities in their own lives?
- Think about a time when you helped someone recognize and act on an opportunity or challenge. In what ways did you succeed? How can you improve your abilities to help someone do that?

DEVELOPING OTHERS

CHAPTER 9

Being a Role Model

As a leader, you are a role model, and everyone is watching. Ensure your words and actions are always aligned.

When you're in a leadership role, it may be tempting to put up a facade to try to appear perfect. This is unwise because at some point, the mask will crumble. In times of stress or difficulty, our true natures have a way of revealing themselves. As a leader, I am always in the spotlight. Because of this, I continually strive to be better. Although I seek to improve myself daily, I also try to be authentic, embracing my core values and beliefs. I am not perfect, and it is okay for those in my organization to see that.

As I mentioned earlier in this book, I started working for my father in our convenience store when I was five years old. Throughout the years, I realized I spent a great deal of time observing how my father conducted himself and paid more attention to his actions than to his verbal instructions. He never asked his employees to do something he wouldn't do himself. Instead, he emphasized the importance of leading by example and being a role model.

Throughout my career, I have kept his practices close to my heart. I strive to be a role model, not for show, but to sincerely demonstrate what it means to be a servant leader. I learned people are always watching you. But even if they aren't, that doesn't mean you can act differently. Betraying your values in private means it's harder to uphold them in public. So I focus on being consistent, no matter the situation, and on being a leader my team is proud to follow.

Over my career in information technology, which has spanned more than three decades, I have worked for great leaders, good leaders, poor leaders, and many in between. While I was influenced by good leaders and taught to stretch by great leaders, I learned the most from the painful experiences of working for poor leaders.

The example I remember most vividly was a manager who was eager to take full credit for any successful project and quick to assign blame when a problem occurred. In one particular instance, a team member's mistake caused an issue, and I ended up in the line of fire even though I was not responsible. The manager didn't investigate the problem and its cause. She simply chose me as the scapegoat. A short time later, I left to pursue another opportunity. That experience taught me that employees don't leave a company; they leave bad leaders.

We cannot choose our challenges in life or in business. We can, however, choose our reactions. I love the Serenity Prayer, composed by Protestant theologian Reinhold Niebuhr.

> God, grant me the serenity to accept the things I cannot change, the courage to change the things I can, and the wisdom to know the difference.

I may not be able to change the circumstances of the challenge, but I can change my attitude. Though it is often difficult, I resolve each day to react positively.

I know my team is watching and that it is up to me to set an example, so I take that responsibility seriously. It isn't important to be perfect. It is important to do your best.

As a servant leader, I frequently remind myself that I'm a role model to my team members. They will learn from my actions and emulate what I do. Therefore, it is important I conduct myself accordingly. If I expect people to do certain things or behave certain ways, I should be willing to model those things first.

I also remind my team that they are role models for other employees within the company. For example, if other teams see our names on the list of projects that are behind schedule, how can we expect them to be on top of their own projects? Therefore, it is important to lead by example and be consistent.

So, in short, since people are watching, you need to figure out how to always be at your best.

- **Be aware.** See yourself for what you really are. Monitor your words and actions carefully, recognize when you make mistakes, and take stock of how you can improve.

- **Be authentic.** Use your core values to guide your daily activities. Do not settle or compromise your standards.

- **Do the right thing.** Carefully consider the situation you're in before taking action and make sure your decisions are in line with your values.

- **Take a positive stance.** Leading a business is challenging, and it is easy to let stress and negative emotions take over. If you maintain a positive attitude, you'll see the good in others and in your organization.

- **Be a role model.** As a leader, you serve as an example, whether you like it or not. Act and speak accordingly.

- **Apologize when you need to.** If you make a mistake, be honest, apologize and then rectify it. Do not sweep the problem under the rug and assume no one will notice.

> Plant the seed of awareness. Reflect on your actions because your team is watching. You want them to see an authentic, positive leader who may not be perfect, but who is constantly striving to improve.

Seedling Reflections: Being a Role Model

Reflect on the qualities of good leadership and how you can set an example for others. Consider each question and write your answers in your journal.

Being authentic

- What does authenticity mean to you?
- Think about a specific experience where you demonstrated authenticity as a leader. In what ways did you demonstrate your values?
- Write about a time when you had to take responsibility for a mistake. What did you learn from it?

Learning from others

- Write about a lesson you learned from a leader you have worked with, whether positive or negative. What did you learn from the experience?
- How have these experiences shaped your leadership style and the way you approach challenges?
- Have you spoken with a mentor about these situations, and what did you learn?

Staying at your best

- Consider the importance of self-awareness in leadership. How does monitoring your words and actions improve your relationships?
- Write about a time when you chose to do the right thing, even if it was difficult. What did you learn from the experience?

Choosing a positive attitude

- Write about a time when you maintained a positive stance in a difficult situation. What impact did that have on your team or organization?

- Which strategies can you use to promote positivity among your team members?

- How does being a role model foster a positive work environment and motivate your team?

CHAPTER 10

Embracing Leadership Styles

An effective leader will push themselves to cultivate those around them, recognizing when someone would benefit more from guidance or independent growth.

Leading an organization presents a complex matrix of challenges: handling daily tactical obligations while creating successful long-term strategies, understanding the overall business landscape, changing priorities based on market movements, and connecting with employees.

It's not uncommon for talent to be limited or deadlines to loom. When that's the case, a leader can ensure success by providing a detailed project roadmap. This includes step-by-step instructions and carefully controlled timelines. I held to this strategy early in my career, because I was focused on completing one project before moving onto the next one.

As I gained more experience, however, I came to realize that controlling every facet of the project was not always the optimal approach. True, sometimes it works and is the best way to get things done. But at other times, a more hands-off management strategy produces better results. It all depends on the team and the project. Leadership is never one size fits all.

For example, when I was just twenty-nine years old and working at a Big Five accounting firm, I was assigned as team lead to rewrite an existing application. All the other team members were between thirty-five and fifty-five years old. When they realized how young I was (and when I realized how "old" they were) their surprise mirrored mine. Several of them voiced concerns about my inexperience.

The first two months were challenging because my leadership ability and decisions were constantly questioned. To get the team on board, I spoke to another senior developer and encouraged him to work with me since we were united in our goal of delivering the project on time. I asked other team members for input and held each individual responsible for our deliverables. As the project moved along, the team became more cohesive, and I saw their respect for the process I had implemented grow. At the end of the project, another senior developer took me aside and told me he was glad I had been the manager.

I could have reacted to the doubts about my leadership abilities by micromanaging the team to show I was capable. Instead, I used what I call the "optimal approach"—allowing the team to help move the project forward by challenging them and harnessing their problem-solving ability.

A project often works best when a leader presents a problem, then gives their team room to create a solution and determine appropriate deadlines. But that isn't always the case.

Therefore, a good leader must be flexible about leadership style. Sometimes, the optimal approach isn't the right fit. It works best if there is a strong team and a long lead time. In other circumstances, a project may require more hands-on management.

When choosing which leadership style to implement, I often let an old Chinese adage guide me: "Give a man a fish and you feed him for a day; teach a man to fish, and you feed him for a lifetime." Sometimes, you can teach your employees to fish. Sometimes, you have no choice but to hand them the fish.

To determine whether you, as a manager, can let your team take the initiative (teaching them to fish) or whether you need to take the lead (giving them a fish), consider the following rubric.

Chapter 10. Embracing Leadership Styles

Encouraging Initiative	Taking the Lead
The project is small and straightforward.	The project is large and complex.
The team size is adequate for the scope of the project.	The team size is insufficient for the scope of the project.
The team is highly skilled.	The team is inexperienced.
The team is seasoned and has worked together for some time.	The team is new.
The timeline is fluid.	The deadline is pressing.

Here are some other tips to consider as you move toward an optimal approach in your management style:

- **Be patient.** Developing talent is a process. Mistakes happen, but encouraging creativity and innovation is worth the hiccups along the way.

- **Have a vision.** Make your goals and expectations clear, and be sure your team understands them. When they know what they're aiming for, they will be more productive.

- **Nurture and guide your team.** Be a willing mentor. A useful suggestion or timely direction can encourage your team and keep the project on track.

- **Know the limitations.** Develop a strong sense of your team's strengths and weaknesses. This will encourage growth without pushing individuals into overwhelming situations. A good leader needs to step in when they see a problem on the horizon.

- **Be mindful of the timing.** Fully understand the project's schedule and clearly communicate it to your team. Do you have the leeway to experiment with a new idea, or is the deadline too unyielding? If time permits, allow the team to go in a new direction—then, if it fails, show them how to measure and adjust.

- **Identify leaders.** As you interact with team members, look for people with strong leadership skills. Spotting and promoting good leaders can transform your organization.

> Plant the seed of evaluating your leadership style. Although your team may accomplish tasks more quickly when you give orders, try to avoid doing so. Instead, by showing patience and listening to different ideas, you can encourage creativity and innovation and ensure your organization thrives.

Seedling Reflections: Embracing Leadership Styles

In your journal, reflect on your recently completed projects and catalog your leadership style for each one.

Assessing your team

- Assess your team's skill level related to the project you're currently working on. Are they experienced and able to brainstorm solutions? Or are they less seasoned, and thus more in need of detailed instructions?

Directing an experienced team

- How will you communicate your vision and goals for this project to your experienced team?
- How will you create a communication plan that outlines how the team will interact with each other?
- What steps will you take to secure agreement for the scope of the work as well as the specific project milestones, responsible parties, and deadlines for each one?
- How will you track the team's progress and adjust plans until you reach your goals?
- How will you celebrate successes with your team? (Think of simple ways, such as bringing in food to share, that can boost morale.)

Managing an inexperienced team

- How will you share a detailed vision of the project with your inexperienced team?

- What is your game plan for the project, and what will each team member be responsible for?

- How will you set firm deadlines for the project?

- What steps will you take to oversee what has been done and provide feedback and guidance?

- How will you celebrate successes in concrete ways with your team?

- How will you monitor progress and adjust the plan as you reach each milestone and ultimately the project goal?

CHAPTER 11

Leading with Influence

Leading others is both a privilege and a responsibility. It is a role you must earn.

There are two hallmarks of leaders: their position and their influence. The first attribute is simply a reflection of the leader's rank or authority over others. The second is due to the relationships they build over time. People trust their example and decisions and are willing to follow them, regardless of whether they hold a management position. Ideally, a leader has both rank and influence.

However, one of the myths in our society is that our needs and wants should be fulfilled with the click of a button. It is the age of instant gratification. Time and experience are crucial elements in developing good managers. Suddenly donning the appropriate title does not automatically bestow the corresponding skills upon you. A kindergartner cannot rush through elementary, intermediate and high school, followed by college, in a year or two. Completing each grade, cementing the foundations of knowledge, and gaining experience are all essential to producing a well-rounded individual. The same is true for leadership. Moving up through a business hierarchy, learning skills, developing vision, exercising patience, and gaining maturity are corners that cannot be cut.

To lead through influence, here are some important skills to develop:

- **Interact with others.** Visit your employees in their workspaces. (That creates a more comfortable environment than having a conversation with them across your desk.) Engage with them to learn who they are, what their interests are, and who their family is. This creates a more holistic understanding of who they are as a person.

- **Show appreciation.** If you genuinely care for your team members, they are more likely to work hard and be responsive. Celebrate their accomplishments and reward their successes. Recognition is key to showing people you care.

- **Invest in training.** Allot time to grow talent within your team. Coach more seasoned employees and mentor less experienced team members. Your education, experience and abilities can be an invaluable resource for others in your organization.

- **Lead by example.** When your actions run counter to your words, your team will cease to trust you. If you make a promise, follow through. If you hold your team to certain expectations, meet them yourself as well.

- **Explain the "why."** It is easier for team members to work hard and commit to a cause if they understand the ramifications. Explain your vision and allow your team to rally around it and move the project forward.

- **Be honest.** It is important to be encouraging, but it is also critical to give effective feedback. Address shortcomings, but do so in a manner that will help team members grow. Honesty helps develop and strengthen relationships.

- **Set challenges.** Seek opportunities to push team members out of their comfort zones. New experiences foster growth and development and can bring your team members' hidden skills to light.

- **Spot talent.** Future leaders must not only be skilled and have vision, but also be passionate and selfless. Be judicious in whom you choose to promote.

Plant the seed of growing talent around you. Be passionate about encouraging others and spend a lot of your free time connecting with team members, fostering relationships between everyone on the team, and developing their skills and capabilities through mentoring, coaching and nurturing. Your goal should be to help your team members reach their true potential.

Seedling Reflections: Leading with Influence

Use the questions in this section to reflect on your approach to leading others. Write your answers in your journal and review them periodically to see if you should make changes.

Communicating with your team

- How do you communicate goals and expectations?
- How do you seek feedback from your team?
- Reflect on your communication style. How might you improve it?

Delegating to others

- How do you delegate tasks and responsibilities to your team members?
- Reflect on your leadership style. How does it empower your team and promote accountability?

Resolving conflict

- Describe a recent conflict you mediated and reflect on how you handled it. What was the outcome?
- Identify any leadership lessons you learned from that situation. How can you improve in the future?

Recognizing and guiding team efforts

- How do you recognize your team members' efforts and provide constructive feedback when things aren't going well?
- How do you celebrate success when your team reaches milestones?
- Reflect on your current approach to recognition and providing feedback to your team. Could it be improved?

Making decisions

- Describe your decision-making approach and reflect on how you might improve it.
- How can you leverage the team's collective wisdom?

Setting goals

- How do you communicate your vision and goals?
- Reflect on the clarity of your shared vision. How do you align your team to your vision and goals?

Encouraging continuous improvement

- Reflect on a situation when you encouraged continuous improvement. What was the outcome?
- How do you facilitate continuous improvement among your team?

Managing team dynamics

- Describe the current dynamics of your team. Reflect on ways to improve them.

- Request input from your stakeholders on the performance of individual team members. Use that feedback to assess how the team is performing. What will you do to make improvements?

CHAPTER 12

Promoting Shared Purpose

*If everyone shares the vision,
it is easier to make progress,
grow and develop.*

As a leader, it is critical to communicate the overarching vision of the organization effectively and bring teams together with a sense of shared purpose. By doing this, you ensure your team not only understands the vision, but also has a personal investment in its success. Ken Blanchard, a business consultant and motivational speaker, reinforces this idea in his book *Leading at a Higher Level*, saying:

> The greatest leaders mobilize others by coalescing people around a shared vision.

There are many techniques a leader can use to help build this sense of unity. During my tenure as an executive director leading a quality assurance organization, we prioritized reinforcing our shared vision by starting each quarterly meeting with a comprehensive review of our team's mission and goals, as well as the current status of each project. Stakeholders in the organization were invited to recognize the team for their contributions to the successful delivery of completed projects.

We maintained this practice for over five years, and each of my direct reports presented the update at one time or another. This approach provided an opportunity for all of us to reaffirm the outcomes we were seeking. The feedback I received verified the value of this practice. Team members expressed appreciation for the grounding effect it had on our collective motivation.

To foster a sense of shared purpose, start by making sure everyone is aware of what the company or team ultimately hopes to achieve. Here are four recommendations to accomplish that:

1. **Clearly articulate the vision.** Use simple descriptions and stories to communicate the outcomes you seek in a concise and understandable manner. Share anecdotes to show the vision in action and progress reports to show how it is attainable.

2. **Use two-way communication.** Engage your team in conversation by asking questions and soliciting answers. Their feedback will ensure the vision resonates with everyone. Listen to your people and address their concerns.

3. **Walk the talk.** Lead by example. Make sure your words and actions are in sync. Demonstrate your commitment with decisions and actions that are consistent and aligned with the vision.

4. **Reinforce the message.** Communicate the vision through all the channels available to you, such as email, meetings and the company website. Repetition helps reinforce the message and keeps the aspiration at the forefront of everyone's minds.

Here are the benefits of making sure everyone is aware of the vision and unified in trying to achieve it.

- **Alignment:** Sharing the vision ensures everyone is working toward the same goal, which promotes alignment within the team or organization.

- **Inspiration and motivation:** A clear and compelling vision inspires team members and fuels their motivation to achieve common objectives. It gives them a sense of purpose and direction and drives them to excel in their roles.

- **Clarity:** When there is clarity about the organization's goals and priorities, team members understand what is expected of them and how their contributions fit into the bigger picture.

- **Empowerment:** Agreement on what the vision is empowers team members to take ownership of their work and make decisions that support the organization's overall goals. This, in turn, fosters a sense of accountability and autonomy.

- **Morale boost:** Team members who understand their contributions have a shared purpose and are more engaged. When morale is high, people do their best work and help the team and organization achieve its goals.

- **Innovation:** A shared vision encourages creativity by providing a framework for exploring new ideas and approaches. It inspires team members to be creative and find innovative solutions to challenges.

The power of shared purpose extends far beyond daily tasks. When individuals understand the "why" behind their work, they are inspired to become the best versions of themselves and are more committed to helping the team or organization achieve its goals.

When I led the quality assurance group, stakeholders frequently provided feedback that my team often went above and beyond what was expected of them. They attributed this to the team's clear understanding of the purpose behind their tasks and their genuine concern for meeting the needs of the stakeholders. When team members recognized the importance of the work we performed, they were fully committed to contributing to the organization's overarching objectives.

Another crucial aspect of creating a shared purpose is the ability to envision what the future holds. As a leader, it's essential to collaborate with your teams to imagine new possibilities for the organization's future, beyond its current financial or market aspirations. This involves developing a roadmap for the organization's evolution—what the future looks like and a plan for how to get there. For example, if you're selling products, it's important to establish a roadmap that outlines how your offerings will evolve over time to meet changing market demands and customer needs. This requires strategic foresight, innovation and alignment with the organization's overall vision and goals. A forward-thinking approach allows leaders to effectively guide their teams toward a successful future and stay ahead of the competition.

> Plant the seed of unified purpose. Consider how you can effectively communicate the company's mission and vision with your team and encourage them to collaborate to realize that purpose in innovative ways. A good leader brings teams together to work with one another in harmony.

Seedling Reflections: Promoting Shared Purpose

Consider which techniques you can use to share the company's vision, inspire shared purpose, and improve motivation among your team members. Respond to these prompts in your journal.

Promoting clarity

- Can you clearly articulate the vision for your organization? Brainstorm some talking points and write those explanations down.
- How can you ensure all the members of your team understand the vision?

Encouraging motivation

- What are some ways you can inspire and motivate your team?
- Can you provide examples of how you've successfully rallied around a shared vision?

Improving communication

- Think about a situation where you've tailored your communication style to your audience. Which techniques did you use?

- Think about some different ways to encourage open dialogue with and feedback from your team, and set goals for implementing them.

Measuring success

- How do you currently measure the success and impact of the shared vision within the organization?

- What do you use to track progress for your team?

- Are these methods effective? Consider why or why not, and brainstorm other solutions if needed.

Ensuring continuous improvement

- How do you ensure the company's vision remains relevant and continues to evolve?

- Share examples of when your team or company has made refinements and improvements. What worked and what did not?

CHAPTER 13

Challenging the Status Quo

*Challenge the norm to create
a better outcome.*

Warren Bennis, who was a professor and scholar of leadership studies, once said, "The manager accepts the status quo; the leader challenges it." In business, we often choose expediency over exactness, and it is easier to follow established practices than to question them and come up with something new. As a result, we miss the chance to develop efficient and sophisticated solutions that fit in better with current trends and thinking.

Years ago, I was asked to recruit candidates at a local college. I was honored to take on the task as I'm passionate about finding and developing talent, and it would allow me to identify and nurture future leaders. During our first recruitment trip, I focused on learning about the process and enjoyed interacting with my peers and interviewing candidates. But as we were evaluating resumes, I realized our organization didn't even consider resumes from students who hadn't met a specific grade point average (GPA) in their classes. I thought to myself, "What if I miss a good candidate who happens to not have an above average GPA?" A strong GPA is an important indicator of success, but as I know from experience, it's not the only indicator.

The next year, I considered every single resume even though it was time-consuming. I looked for unique qualities and experiences that jumped out at me—not just at the applicant's grades. After many hours of reading, I had a strong selection of resumes.

If I'd used the prior recruiter's usual GPA cutoff, my pile would have been much smaller, but I was happy with the outcome, and the process moved along smoothly.

One candidate whose GPA was below our typical standard impressed me with his personal story, dedication and commitment to improving. We hired him as an intern that year. The next year, we brought him back, and we worked on a more challenging project together. He was proactive and diligent about his work, so at the end of his internship, we hired him and offered him a spot in our management training program. He went on to work for almost five years with the company and even earned a promotion along the way.

Now, whenever I see him, it reminds me that deciding to challenge the status quo yielded excellent results. I also remember that every person has circumstances we know nothing about, and if you take the opportunity to listen to their story, you may see them in a new light.

Efficient organizations develop specific processes as solutions to the problems they face every day. These established patterns ensure the company's success. However, I often find myself questioning whether we are following these routines because they guarantee the best outcome or if we've fallen into a habit of repeating what we've done in the past.

It is tempting to continue doing things the old way because it saves time and achieves dependable results. However, that approach has some downsides, including:

- developing solutions that might not be a good fit.

- sidestepping or ignoring current technology.

- failing to maximize features in order to shorten development time.

- not fully educating people or developing their talents.

- making projects inefficient and forcing them to be reworked.

Following an established process makes sense, but so does regularly reviewing that pattern to make sure it still fits our needs. I have learned to step back and postpone making judgments or decisions until I better understand what our goals are. In addition, I challenge the people on my team to assess our established process and ensure we're using the best development model. This helps my team adjust plans accordingly.

Challenging the status quo happens in myriad ways. It is essential to help your business differentiate itself and ensure success. At times, it involves a small decision with little noticeable impact; at others, it leaves a long-term legacy. Either way, it is an essential step in growing your business and developing your talents.

> Plant the seed of challenging the status quo and continue to do so by asking yourself, "Must things stay the same, or can we make them better by changing our approach?"

Seedling Reflections: Challenging the Status Quo

It is often easier to go along with what has been done before rather than break the mold and start down a new path. But we do ourselves, our team members, and our organization a disservice by not considering innovative approaches.

In this exercise, think about situations in which doing something different could be beneficial and record your answers in your journal.

Learning from the past

- What has contributed to your successes? What did you learn from them? Are there things you can do differently?

- How about your failures? What did you learn from them? Are there things you can do differently?

Identifying issues and solutions

- What current issues might lend themselves to new solutions? Make a list. This might involve a current project or a personnel issue.

- What are some potential solutions? Think about how each one will help solve the problem in a new way, and then imagine the problems that solution could create. Repeat the process for each solution you've come up with.

Working your action plan

- What is your most promising solution? Create an action plan to implement it. Make it time-bound and track your progress. Check your progress every two weeks and review and adjust accordingly.

- During every check in, consider whether your new approach is working. Write down why it is or isn't. What have you learned? And how can you apply this information to problems that come up in the future?

CHAPTER 14

Nurturing Others

Elevating talented people makes us stronger and better. Dedicate time to mentoring potential leaders in your circle.

There came a point in my career when I realized I needed to learn more about what it takes to be the leader I wanted to be. That's when I made the decision to return to school to attend the executive program at Seton Hall. At that point, I consciously set aside time to develop the talent around me as well because I believe people are our most important asset. To increase an organization's overall capabilities, we must invest in our employees. If we do that, they are more likely to do their best when serving our clients. It's a win-win situation.

But individuals may not fully recognize their own potential. As a leader, it's essential you actively seek out talent within your organization and be willing to invest in their development. Take Cynthia, for instance. She reported to me within a quality assurance organization and was a subject matter expert in a specific business area for over eleven years. Upon closer interaction, I saw she had a remarkable ability to learn. Notably, she also commanded the respect of her peers. When she spoke, they listened.

After a year with the team, I believed it was time for her to venture into another related domain within my organization that had greater responsibilities. When I shared this idea with Cynthia, she expressed uncertainty about whether she could handle it. I assured her she would have my unwavering support at every step, emphasized her capabilities, and expressed my belief in her potential.

Despite her initial hesitation, she accepted the opportunity. Over the next six months, I guided her through the journey, witnessing her impressive growth and hearing business partners express their gratitude for her contributions. Her confidence flourished, and within a year, she became the go-to person in her new area. Our partners valued her opinions, and her performance garnered notice outside our team.

After less than two years of preparation, Cynthia was promoted. Her success is just one example of the remarkable progress achieved by individuals within our organization during my tenure in that role.

In order to guide Cynthia through the transition from her comfort area to taking on greater responsibility, we created a comprehensive, personalized, talent development process. That plan comprised these key elements:

- **Goals and aspirations:** Encourage individuals to take responsibility for their career journeys and emphasize the importance of continual learning and yearly growth.

- **Current state:** Identify where individuals are in their career journey.

- **Target state requirements:** Together, outline the skills, experience and competence needed for the candidate to achieve their goals.

- **Gap analysis:** Evaluate the candidate's strengths as well as areas where they need improvement. Then identify their accomplishments so far, as well as what they still need to do to meet the target state requirements.

- **Value addition:** Assess how each individual contributed to the team and the organization beyond their daily duties. Then identify the skills they need to differentiate themselves from other candidates and the opportunities for growth.

- **Plan of action:** After completing the previous steps, define the key actions and training needed to propel the individual to the next level. Then set specific, time-bound and realistic action plans and assigned accountability partners.

- **Assessment of progress:** Review the plan multiple times throughout the year with the individual to track their development and make adjustments if necessary.

Over a seven-year period, we promoted an average of ten individuals annually due to using this strategy at one company I worked with. Yet, our focus transcended mere promotions. We cultivated a culture where individuals actively engaged in shaping their personalized career plans.

As the saying goes, "If you don't have a plan, chances are you're working on someone else's plan." The emphasis in this program was on proactively crafting professional journeys to ensure a potential leader's plans are in alignment with their personal aspirations, not just the needs of the business.

> Plant the seed of developing the talent of others around you. Constantly seek out individuals who have potential and the right skills. Support their hopes and dreams, and in turn, your organization will thrive.

Seedling Reflections: Nurturing Others

As leaders, it is crucial to provide team members with opportunities to shine, offering training and support along the way and allowing them to grow stronger each day. Answer these prompts in your journal to enhance your ability to spot and nurture talent.

Developing an eye for talent

- Are you aware of those around you? To develop an eye for talent, you need to genuinely care for your team members and make a habit of reviewing their work.
- What are some ways you can evaluate your team members' work and recognize them for their efforts?

Benefiting from mentorship

- How have you been nurtured in your career? Make a list of your mentors. Beside their names, describe how they shaped and guided you.
- If you have never had a mentor, seek one out. In your journal, make a list of potential candidates who might mentor you. Then, choose one and ask whether they would be willing to establish specific meeting times and set and review goals. Plan an agenda for each session and afterward summarize your discussion. Create an action plan based on your conversation. Set a date for a follow-up appointment to discuss your progress and set additional goals.
- Choose one person in your organization to mentor. Learn all you can about this person and help them further their goals. Who did you choose, and how will you help them?
- Keep a journal of your efforts to nurture the talents and skills of others. As you document your work, you'll see how mentoring bears fruit, which will inspire you to continue.

CHAPTER 15

Maintaining Relevance

The key to lasting success in leadership is maintaining your relevance as times evolve.

Remember your first leadership position and the excitement that went along with it? Many people feel like they've achieved a major goal when that happens. You may be tempted to think, *Whew! I've arrived!* Sadly, resting on your laurels is not an option. A good leader must be able to sustain their success. This means maintaining a higher level of performance.

The skills that make you a leader today may be very different from the ones the company will need tomorrow. In a rapidly changing world, businesses are constantly evolving and being confronted with new challenges. Global economies add another layer of complexity. Political or economic ripples in a country thousands of miles away can drastically affect markets at home. A good leader must be able to respond quickly and efficiently to new developments. They need to have the foresight to see problems coming and craft solutions before those problems can have a significant negative impact.

Throughout my career, I have focused on maintaining my ability to remain relevant to the work at hand. By this, I mean staying current and being able to tackle the work or challenges in front of us. Whether it's technical or nontechnical, I always recommend conducting a year-end strategy meeting with your direct reports to review your challenges and opportunities, and then developing a plan to navigate the year ahead. This practice allows us to stay on top of the situation.

This approach has also opened the eyes of my direct reports to the importance of looking ahead and gaining relevant skills early, before it becomes an emergency, and enables them to prepare and plan accordingly. It helps them understand the risks our team takes on so they can devise new strategies to sustain our performance.

Here are some questions you might ask yourself as you consider the future of your organization:

- What challenges is your organization facing?
- What are the key risks that may affect your organization's ability to compete in the marketplace?
- Are you comfortable with creating a mitigation plan?

As you consider these questions, do an honest self-assessment regarding whether you have the knowledge to solve a given problem. If you do, consider who else in your organization also needs to be trained to deal with the issue and how much time you have to complete that training. If you don't feel prepared, don't panic. Decide what you need to learn and the best way to master the necessary skills. Is there a training program or book that would help (and do you have time for such an undertaking)? Does someone within your organization have the skills? Can you pull that person onto your team to bring a fresh perspective to the problem?

Remind yourself that challenges are opportunities. A leader's success rests partly on their ability to adapt to change, and guiding your organization successfully through a difficult period is a chance for you to shine. This includes embracing change by understanding the rationale behind it and leading your team through it successfully.

> Plant the seed of relevance by looking to the future and understanding the challenges that lie ahead for your industry. Your goal is to keep up with the demands of your position and consistently and successfully guide the organization over a long time.

Seedling Reflections: Maintaining Relevance

As a leader, it is important to prepare yourself for the future, so your work and skills remain valuable. Reflect on these questions to identify your strengths in this area and where you might improve. Write your answers in your journal.

Benchmarking the industry

- What current and future trends do you see in your sector?
- Where are you in comparison to these trends?
- How can you take advantage of the opportunities you identify?

Future proofing

- How do you equip your team for upcoming opportunities and challenges?
- Write about a strategy you've implemented that enabled your team to be ready for future challenges. What was it, and how did it help your organization?

Encouraging resilience

- Consider ways in which you can cultivate resilience within yourself and for your team. Write down these ideas for reference later.

- Which tactics have you used to help your team navigate challenges? How successful were they? How can you improve next time?

- Reflect on one key lesson you've learned from implementing resilience strategies. What is it, and what makes it significant to you?

LOOKING TO THE FUTURE

CHAPTER 16

Changing of the Guard

It will eventually be time for you to move on. A leader must help their team prepare for the future.

Several times in my career, I have seen leaders step aside to allow a new generation to take the helm. These individuals wisely recognized the need for change and saw that younger leaders would take the organization to the next level. Although most of this book is about improving your leadership of a team, there will inevitably come a time when you will need to move on. Perhaps you are ready to take on new challenges, or the team is going in a different direction and you see that a distinct skill set from your own is needed for success. Whatever the case may be, a good leader pays attention to this evolution and makes succession plans.

Years ago, I accepted a very challenging management position where I was asked to lead a team of developers who had been unable to deliver a product successfully. The client was frustrated, the previous managers had left the firm, and morale was low.

When I stepped in, I began by listening intently to both the client and my team of developers. I sought to understand the client's needs and the frustrations of my team so we could create a viable solution. I wanted the client to understand I was committed to delivering the solution they expected and the team to understand I wasn't there just to bark orders, but to work alongside them.

After five months of tireless effort, we released the first version of the product. The client was happy, and after two other successful releases, they were thrilled. After that first release, however, I was asked to manage another group, so I began thinking about who would take over after I left to ensure the team would continue to function seamlessly. I identified a new potential leader and quietly started giving him more responsibility so he could easily take my place. My goal wasn't just a win in terms of one project. I had the long-term success of the group in mind. I wanted them to function well in my absence and sought to create an environment in which this could occur.

Being a leader is not an end state. The torch may be passed for many reasons: personal issues, retirement or the good of the company. It is essential to the organization's overall progress that its leader knows when to step aside. I have mentioned in earlier chapters that a leader needs to be selfless. Passing the torch is the ultimate demonstration of selflessness.

In such cases, succession planning is crucial. If a leader has nurtured and developed team members along the way, those individuals will be ready for additional responsibilities. When the time is right, the departing leader can assist with the transition and simply remain available for future guidance and mentoring.

> Plant the seed of recognizing the opportunity for change. Move on when the time is right and consider what is best for yourself and your organization. As Denzel Washington wrote in his book *A Hand to Guide Me*:
>
> > At the end of the day, it's not about what you have or even what you've accomplished. It's about what you've done with those accomplishments. It's about who you've lifted up, who you've made better. It's about what you've given back.
>
> Leadership is about giving back.

Seedling Reflections: Changing of the Guard

Are you actively seeking future leaders for your team? Use these prompts to create an action plan for identifying those who have leadership capabilities that will help your organization grow. In your journal, write down the names of the individuals you've chosen and how you can nurture their talent and potential.

Reflecting on leadership

- Think about the qualities that make you the leader you are. Which of these are critical for your position and should be used as criteria for choosing an individual to fill your role?

- Identify key talent—people whom you can see as future leaders. Why are they suitable candidates?

Nurturing future leaders

- Spend one-on-one time with your key talent. What drives them? What is their passion? What do they want to achieve? How can you nurture their talent so they grow as individuals and as team members?

- Assign these individuals specific projects to see how they respond to the demands of leadership. What upcoming tasks and responsibilities would be a good fit for them?

- Over time, observe the people you have selected in action and narrow the list to one or two team members who would be best suited to take over your role. Who are they, and why did you pick them?

Planning for the future

- Which responsibilities can you delegate to these individuals when the time comes?

- Brainstorm goals with these individuals and schedule follow-up meetings to review their progress. What are their targets, and when will you discuss them?

- Which of your duties are critical and how will you train your successor on them?
- Consider the signs you will need to see before deciding that it's the right time to transition roles. What indicators will you use to make your decision?

CHAPTER 17

Moving Forward after Setbacks

Setbacks are part of life's journey. Embrace the opportunity to learn and grow.

Whenever I face a challenge, I call to mind a quote from Robin Sharma, a Canadian author and founder of Sharma Leadership International. He says, "The beautiful thing about setbacks is that they introduce us to our strengths." I have faced many setbacks on my journey, and they often caused me to doubt myself and eroded my confidence. However, when handled properly, setbacks can fuel our desire to improve and create a better version of ourselves.

When I was in high school, my class was divided into three sections. The first consisted of all the top students, and the other sections comprised the remainder. I did not make it into the first section during my freshman year. My parents were disappointed because my brother had been in the first section for all four years of high school. I was sad about it, but I decided to use the setback as an opportunity to learn and did not let it extinguish my desire to improve myself.

Despite failing to make the first section for the next two years, I stayed focused and resilient, with a goal of making it in during my senior year. Finally, as my junior year came to a close, I finished third in my section, which enabled me to move to the first section for my senior year. I was proud of my achievement. It had taken me longer than anyone else in my family, but I proved to myself I could do it.

What did I learn from this setback? If you want something badly enough, you will work hard and persevere until you succeed. I focused on making incremental improvements that brought me closer to my goal each year. I also learned that although it took longer to reach my goal, I cherished my accomplishment more. Life is a marathon, not a sprint, and we are not running at the same pace. Ultimately, it is not about how you start, but rather how you finish.

When I was applying to colleges, studying at De La Salle University (DLSU) in Manila was something I had always dreamed of, but at the time I was not sure what I wanted to study. So I followed my friend's example and took an entrance test for mechanical engineering. Unfortunately, when the results came out, I'd failed—another setback in my journey. Despite this, I vowed that one day, I would study at that school.

As a teenager, I dreamed of studying architecture, but my parents believed I lacked the aptitude for it. They insisted I study commerce instead, which they deemed easier. To please them, I took the entrance exam at the University of Santo Tomas, also in Manila, passed the admission test, and subsequently enrolled in the College of Commerce. I majored in accounting and took some programming courses, where I discovered my love for computer science.

About a year after I got my first software developer job, I decided to take the entrance exam for an MBA at DLSU. While I had failed to secure admission to the undergraduate program, I had learned a lot in seven years. I was methodical in preparing for the exam. In fact, there was extra pressure for me to pass because my brother decided to take the same exam also. When the results came out, I was elated to discover we both had passed and been accepted into the DLSU graduate program.

I learned from this experience that setbacks are temporary. It reminds me of a quote from Robert T. Kiyosaki, author of the *Rich Dad, Poor Dad* personal finance book series:

> Failure is part of the process of success. People who avoid failure also avoid success.

Chapter 17. Moving Forward after Setbacks

That was why I embraced the opportunity to learn and discover my strength through perseverance.

In my career, I've had my share of missed opportunities for promotion. In one instance, I was passed over two years in a row. Instead of lamenting and complaining about why I hadn't gotten promoted, I asked for specific feedback I could use to improve. At times, it is difficult to hear that you did not make it again. But it didn't mean I wasn't capable. It just meant I needed more time to improve. It's about trusting the process. To achieve something worthwhile takes time.

In the end, I needed to unlearn something I had grown up with as part of Chinese culture: my father had taught me that I should focus on doing good work and, if I did so, my manager would then recognize my efforts and reward me. But I learned that as you climb the management ranks, you need to share with others what your team is doing and the value they are producing. That was not something I was comfortable with, so I had to unlearn my father's lesson, and instead share what my team does with all our stakeholders. By presenting our work to everyone, in addition to doing great work, I finally earned my promotion.

In this situation, the lesson I learned was to always ask for feedback, seek help to guide me through the process, and finally, be patient because sometimes it will not happen for days, weeks or even months. Sometimes, it takes years.

To develop resilience, here are some suggestions on how to change your perspective:

- Ask for specific feedback from those you trust in positions of management above you and whom you work with. Focus on the scenario and seek help to improve.

- Share their feedback with your mentor or coach and ask for their guidance and support.

- Sometimes, you need to unlearn something and do something new.

- Getting to the next level does not just mean doing a good job. It's about how you differentiate yourself from everyone else in the pack.

- Don't be discouraged. Trust the process, as long as you have a specific improvement you're working on.

- Keep believing in yourself. It is easy to be discouraged when you see others receiving promotions. Cheer them on. Your day will come.

- Don't assume your manager knows what you want or that they will take care of you. You alone are responsible for your career.

- Be ready to learn lessons and don't waste time lamenting why you missed an opportunity.

- Be disciplined. Do not give up, and work toward your goals every day.

- A setback is temporary, but giving up makes it permanent. The choice is yours.

- Remember, a setback prepares you for a better tomorrow.

Plant the seed of learning from setbacks and forging your path forward. Through continuous learning and growth, you can work toward your goals. It is important to recognize setbacks are part of our journey, serving as reminders that we are a work in progress. They highlight that the best is yet to come and motivate us to persevere.

Seedling Reflections: Moving Forward after Setbacks

Answer these questions in your journal to reflect on setbacks you've experienced and how you can learn from them, then develop strategies for moving forward.

Acknowledging setbacks

- Describe a recent setback you faced on your leadership journey.
- How did you initially react to the setback?

Understanding the impacts

- Describe the effect of the setback on you, your team, or your organization.
- What key lessons or insights did you gain from this experience?

Embracing the learning opportunity

- How has this setback changed you?
- What are three lessons you learned from the experience?

Making a plan

- Outline actionable steps for overcoming the setback.
- Set specific goals and a timeline for moving forward.
- Track and monitor your progress.

Soliciting feedback

- How have you sought support from your mentor during challenges you've experienced?
- How has seeking feedback helped you improve?

CHAPTER 18

Acknowledging Others

Recognition is the vital fuel that propels individual contributors forward within a strong team, creating unstoppable momentum and igniting success in every aspect of their journey.

Early in my career, I was tasked with upgrading a software application. As a new manager in the company, I was eager to demonstrate my ability to get the job done. Consequently, I was hyperfocused on making progress according to our plan, to the extent that I began micromanaging everyone's work. Despite the team making great progress, morale was low. As days turned into weeks and then months, it became apparent that the team was not functioning as well as I had hoped.

Fortunately, we completed the project six weeks ahead of the deadline. However, when I asked each team member if they wanted to work on my next initiative, I was surprised to find that no one was interested. I couldn't understand why they wouldn't want to work with a successful manager.

Over the next two weeks, as I sought new members for my next project, I took time to reflect and speak to each member from the previous team. All of them indicated I had been overly focused on meeting the deadline. They felt their effort had gone unrecognized by management once the goal was achieved, despite exceeding expectations. I apologized to every one of them and vowed to learn from the experience to avoid making similar mistakes in the future.

Based on the lesson I learned, I made sure to do two things going forward: take time to recognize the people who worked hard on the project and to celebrate the team's successes. I make it a point now to mark every milestone as well as the final accomplishment.

My determination to do this is reinforced by one of my favorite quotes from Oprah Winfrey, which appears in a 1986 edition of the news magazine *Jet*:

> The more you praise and celebrate your life, the more there is in life to celebrate. The more you complain, the more you find fault, the more misery and fault you will have to find.

Acknowledging individuals for their contributions and successes has a positive effect on the employee, the team, and the organization as a whole. Here are some of the benefits:

- Morale boosting
  - Recognizing and celebrating success serves as a powerful motivator and increases team spirit. It can also inspire people to continue to put in their best effort.
  - Positive reinforcement encourages people to be proactive about future work.
- Increased job satisfaction
  - Feeling appreciated and acknowledged contributes to higher job satisfaction.
  - Recognizing employees makes them more likely to stay engaged and can foster a positive work environment.

- Improved employee retention

  - People who feel valued are more likely to stay with the company.

  - Recognition contributes to a sense of loyalty, and hence reduces turnover and associated costs.

- Increased productivity

  - Improving retention contributes to more productive teams because they are familiar with similar completed projects.

  - People who feel recognized tend to strive for excellence because they know they'll be rewarded accordingly.

- Positive reputation

  - Recognizing teams or people for their accomplishments is more likely to build a higher regard for the company and attract a larger workforce.

  - A positive image can help attract customers and affects the company's brand and reputation.

- Employee loyalty

  - Employees who feel cared for and recognized will dedicate themselves to their work.

  - Increasing employee loyalty can impact the organization's brand and reputation.

In summary, when you celebrate success and recognize individuals, it benefits not only that individual but the organization as a whole. It creates a positive culture, increases productivity, and contributes to the organization's long-term success.

How can you create a framework for celebrating success?

- Intentionally look for opportunities to celebrate and recognize people.

- As you make progress on a project, look for and recognize those who go above and beyond.

- When you achieve a particular milestone, take the time to congratulate everyone, perhaps with a small get-together, such as buying pizza to celebrate the occasion.

- When you deliver a key initiative, celebrate it with recognition at a company gathering, perhaps presented by stakeholders.

- Consider incorporating rewards and incentives for exceptional performance into your standard practice. You could offer monetary bonuses, gift cards, or extra days off to reinforce the value of outstanding contributions.

- Finally, encourage your people to recognize their fellow team members for their contributions.

> Plant the seed of celebrating success and offering recognition. Make it a regular practice in your leadership journey.

Seedling Reflections: Acknowledging Others

Focusing on opportunities to celebrate success and offer recognition is essential for fostering a positive and motivated work environment. How are you recognizing the achievements of your team members and the goals they accomplish? Consider these questions and their corresponding recommendations and how they might work within your organization.

Fostering a culture of recognition

- How can you build recognition into your organization's culture? Could you establish a forum in which individuals can nominate their peers for an "Above and Beyond" award or a "Making a Difference" award?

- How can you make recognition a regularly scheduled event? Could you implement a quarterly meeting to acknowledge both team-wide and individual accomplishments in reaching key outcomes? What are some other ideas?

- How can you ensure that recognition is thoughtful and specific, highlighting distinct contributions and the impact they had on the team or organization?

CHAPTER 19

Putting It All Together

Just like a puzzle, you determine how each piece of your leadership journey fits. But to start, you first need to know what picture you're painting. So start with the end in mind. What do you want your leadership to look like?

As a leader, the sweetest success is found in developing your people and seeing them grow to the point where they can move on and lead others. During my professional life, spanning over three decades, I have chosen many times to support the promotion of my direct reports.

For example, in 2008, I had a direct report working on one of my critical projects. An opportunity became available, and he was approached to gauge his interest. I'd mentored and coached him for many years, and he came to me to discuss the opportunity, expressing his desire to take it on. I knew that if he left, my team would suffer, resulting in a lot of work for the rest of us to cover. But after thinking about the choice and about his greater good, I encouraged him to take the opportunity, which ended up leading to his promotion.

I did the exact same thing in 2021 when I entrusted Cynthia, who I mentioned in an earlier chapter, with the responsibility of overseeing the quality assurance organization. I have consistently sought to empower my team members, allowing them to seize opportunities and bask in the success and recognition that follow. A selfless leadership style not only fosters individual growth but also cultivates leadership within the team over time.

Integrity, honesty, responsibility, accountability, loyalty and commitment are the hallmarks of good leaders. These qualities can help you form a strong foundation, but what you initially emulate from others, you eventually need to develop on your own to form your own leadership style. At some point, you need to be you.

In this book, we've explored the steps to becoming your own type of leader and I've encouraged you to reflect on these steps in your own journal or the downloadable PDF I provided at emeraldlakebooks.com/SLpdf. By writing things down, you can go back and look at them again over time to see the progress that you made.

Let's briefly revisit each of the steps we covered.

To begin, you need to start by knowing yourself first (Chapter 1. Knowing Yourself). What better way to do that than by exploring your own traits? Once you've assessed your strengths and weaknesses, you can amplify the former while working on the latter. Remember to enhance your strengths continually!

Next, to succeed in leading others, you need to have confidence in yourself (Chapter 2. Valuing Yourself). Therefore, you need to work on valuing yourself—believing in your abilities and granting sufficient time and energy to give new things a try.

As I think about this topic, I remember a quote often attributed to Dale Carnegie:

> Don't be afraid to give your best to what seemingly are small jobs. Every time you conquer one, it makes you that much stronger. If you do the little jobs well, the big ones will tend to take care of themselves.

This quote resonates with me because I've had to take baby steps and tackle challenges one at a time until I developed my self-confidence and climbed out of the shadow of how other people see me and my capabilities. Without overcoming self-doubt, it will be an uphill battle for you to lead others.

Character plays an important role in the longevity of an organization (Chapter 3. Developing Character). If you have great leaders that commit to doing the right thing no matter what, chances are the company will successfully attain its goal.

We need leaders who don't compromise, settle or place their agendas ahead of the company's. We also need to develop individuals who will lead by using their core values and sticking to them. This is by far the most challenging aspect of planting the seeds of better leadership. Make sure you're surrounded by people who are grounded and honest. You don't want yes-men and folks who practice groupthink!

To ensure you're improving as a leader, you must measure your progress. Self-assessment makes you accountable (Chapter 4. Assessing Yourself). Although a leader is often their own worst critic, without tracking your progress, it's difficult to ensure you are actually making any! Self-assessment is a useful tool to determine your baseline and come up with action plans and specific target dates to move you in the right direction. The data you gather and evaluate will be valuable, as you can continue to improve on your strengths while working on your weaknesses. I would recommend you do this at least once a quarter to continually develop your overall capabilities.

Having a firm grasp on your priorities is another seed of growing strong leadership (Chapter 5. Setting Priorities). If you don't know your intentions, it's like climbing a ladder, only to realize you're in the wrong place. Understanding the objectives of both the company and yourself is very important because you can align the two and focus on activities that contribute to attaining the goal. This is referred to as "investing in yourself" or "reaping what you sow." If you really understand your priorities, then when a conflicting request for your time comes up, you can make objective decisions to propel you toward success.

To improve as a leader, be a lifelong student (Chapter 6. Becoming an Active Learner). But saying you read something doesn't mean you understood it. You must apply your learning properly. I've taken many courses and thought to myself afterward that I would use my newfound knowledge, only to fall back into my old, familiar habits. Now, to avoid this, I force myself to apply what I learn each day. By being persistent with this, I have been able to develop habits that enable me to use the same knowledge to help others.

It is important to realize you begin with learning and then transition to understanding. After that, you can challenge and expand the ideas you have learned and come up with use cases in which to apply them. When you are persistent, you'll habitually apply your new knowledge. That is when you can really say you're a leader: when you lead others using the knowledge you have learned and applied.

Continuous improvement is vital to your ability to develop new leaders (Chapter 7. Improving Continuously). Therefore, you must commit to lifelong learning. It is by this means that you will be able to help others. With the knowledge you gain, you can develop more leaders. Your dedication to continuous improvement ensures you are always assisting others and adapting to ever-changing market needs.

You must also be ready to seize opportunities as they arise (Chapter 8. Seizing the Moment). The best preparation for tomorrow is doing the work today. You must plan what you want to do, take action, and track your progress.

Does this sound like taking an assessment? It's not. An assessment is when you map your baseline; this is acting on your plan. You must not wait for an opportunity and only then realize you don't have what it takes to seize the moment. Prepare now, so when the opportunity presents itself, you'll be ready.

After developing our inner skills, it's time to pay attention to our outward-facing talents. When you step into a leadership role, people will always be watching you (Chapter 9. Being a Role Model). The people who work with and follow you are observing how you conduct yourself and will take their cues from you. You will be put to the test because your actions will speak louder than your words. Be self-aware and make sure you do the right thing. Always take a positive stance, make sure to look on the bright side, learn from your mistakes, and see the good in others. Don't let an isolated incident dominate your day. Remember, you can't pick or choose what you will face in life, but you are responsible for how you respond to the situations you encounter. Therefore, you need to always do your best.

When you seek to develop future leaders, be sure to choose the right approach (Chapter 10. Embracing Leadership Styles). At times, you may need to tell people what to do, but don't rely on that continuously because that will not help the business. After all, as soon as you become too busy, you will no longer have the time to tell your people what to do and they will be stuck waiting for your instructions. You will become the bottleneck, effectively blocking your team's progress. Instead, learn to empower people so they can be responsible for their own work and become the organization's future leaders.

As Steve Jobs said:

> It doesn't make sense to hire smart people and then tell them what to do. We hire smart people so they can tell us what to do.

In the end, the smart people you hire and develop as leaders will, in turn, increase your organization's overall capabilities and improve its competitive advantage.

Assessing the capabilities of your people is essential. Once you know which people to develop, resist the temptation to tell them what to do and instead challenge them to think creatively and come up with solutions to help the company differentiate itself from its competitors.

When deciding how to lead, also consider where your authority is coming from (Chapter 11. Leading with Influence). Were you simply placed in a leadership role, or have you worked your way up and gained the respect of your peers? Knowing this will help you decide how to move forward with your team and choose appropriate strategies to strengthen your position. Although it is sometimes inevitable that we are placed into a leadership role, we can always work to acquire the skills we need to be inspiring and effective leaders.

A potent driving force in any organization is whether leaders can articulate and share their vision and then rally the team around it (Chapter 12. Promoting Shared Purpose). It's vital for individuals within the organization to comprehend how their work contributes to overarching goals. Clearly explaining the "why" behind a task or objective is essential. When people understand the "why," they are motivated to give their best effort to achieving the organization's goals. Having them align with the vision can boost morale and ignite innovation. Remember, alignment leads to better outcomes.

However, you must be prepared to challenge the status quo (Chapter 13. Challenging the Status Quo). I've often heard the comment, "We've been doing it this way for many years." Or, "If it ain't broke, don't fix it." If we always listen to ideas like those, we will never make any progress.

Imagine if we had started in the Stone Age and never reinvented or changed things! Challenging the status quo means doing what is right rather than going with the flow and sticking to groupthink. Just because many people agree to do something a certain way doesn't mean it's the best way. Always seek the most beneficial approach. Just keep in mind that you also need to be practical—you shouldn't dream up something that cannot be implemented or will cost an exorbitant amount.

With increasing demand and the challenge of doing more with less, we as leaders are called upon to be more efficient and focus on productivity. However, you can only squeeze so much. At some point, nothing else will come out. Therefore, it is best to focus on developing the talent around you to enable your firm to increase its overall capacity (Chapter 14. Nurturing Others). Raising leaders creates multiplying factors. These leaders will then grow the next generation of leaders, who, in turn, can produce even more leaders.

The key to maintaining relevance is to look forward and future proof yourself (Chapter 15. Maintaining Relevance). We should continually evaluate our skills and assess whether they are what our organization will need in the future, and if not, make a plan to acquire those skills. It's also important to recognize that, as leaders, we should feel comfortable seeking assistance when needed. We aren't expected to have all the answers or be experts in every aspect of our roles. It's perfectly acceptable to admit we have things we need to work on.

A leader also knows when to manage and when it's time to let others step up (Chapter 16. Changing of the Guard). You won't lead your group forever. You need to recognize when it is time for others to take your spot. At that point, you'll move on and pursue new opportunities.

It is a difficult situation to be in, but a leader must be selfless and aim to serve others. You need to think in terms of being a caretaker—nothing is permanent. The best gift you can give your team is the lessons you've shared and the time you've spent with them. Be generous in sharing your time and make sure to focus on succession planning. A good leader always thinks about the future. Leaving a legacy for others to follow and gifting them with knowledge that enables them and their people to carry on will elevate the organization as a whole.

In your journey toward becoming a better leader, you are bound to encounter failure and setbacks (Chapter 17. Moving Forward after Setbacks). How you navigate these situations ultimately shapes the outcome. During challenging times, you need to look for guidance and support. It's important to recognize being an effective leader doesn't require you to have all the answers. Each setback you face is an opportunity to learn something new, which ultimately helps you become a better leader.

And finally, it's critical to pay attention to when goals and milestones have been achieved, our team's as well as our own (Chapter 18. Acknowledging Others). Celebrating milestones is essential to ensuring our team members feel recognized for their efforts, boosting morale and improving the overall culture of the company. Don't fall into the trap of always rushing to check off the next thing on the to-do list. Instead, come up with ways that meaningfully recognize team members for their accomplishments and celebrate the team's success.

At the beginning of this book, we set out to establish some guidelines for how to become a good leader. Ultimately, it is up to you to follow these suggestions and implement them. Through study and application, you'll both differentiate yourself and improve your abilities.

Remember, planting the seeds to be a better leader will make you valuable to any organization you work with and, more importantly, will allow you to reap what you sow.

Thank you for reading *Seeds of Leadership*. If you've enjoyed this book, please share it with your friends and leave a review on your favorite review site. This will help me reach more readers who may benefit from reading it. Remember, we can develop one leader at a time, then they, in turn, can develop many more leaders to help your organization grow!

Author's Note

After over thirty years serving as a leader, I've come to understand that being fully present in the moment is a crucial skill. It allows you to capitalize on every opportunity that comes your way. However, taking advantage of too many opportunities is the surest way to burn out.

As leaders, we are often taught to be self-sacrificing, which can lead us to prioritize others at the expense of our own well-being. However, this approach can ultimately result in burnout. It is crucial for us to establish healthy boundaries and recognize that in order to effectively support others, we must first take care of ourselves. Remember the old saying: "You cannot pour from an empty cup." Don't neglect the important aspects of your life. Always keep in mind that health is wealth and maintain a clear perspective. Once a moment has passed, it can never be retrieved, so cherish each moment and prioritize self-care.

When I found myself at a professional crossroad one February morning while writing this book, I woke up very early and could not go back to sleep because many ideas were swirling through my brain. In those moments, as I reflected on my journey, I was inspired to write this poem, which reflects the ebb and flow of leadership. It encapsulates life's essence in a few stanzas.

In the Blink of an Eye

We rise each day, tasks at hand, goals to chase.
Some days bring triumph, in others, we need grace.
Days turn into weeks, the months unfold.
We celebrate milestones, stories untold.

Setbacks and failures, they may discourage,
But we choose to learn and let them encourage.
Investing in people, the key to success.
Together we strive, overcoming distress.

In the space of a second, everything can change.
What once was possible may seem out of range.
If we could rewind time, what would we do?
Reflect on the past? Seek a different view?

Nothing is permanent, a truth we can't deny.
Life is short, and swiftly flies by.
So embrace each day for what it may bring,
Opportunities from our hard work may spring.

Focus on helping, make a meaningful impact.
Hold on to the present, slipping through the cracks.
The moments pass by, never to return.
So cherish them dearly, each in their turn.

Stay in the moment. Seize each passing day.
For in the blink of an eye, time slips away.

Acknowledgments

To my daughters, Faith and Maddy: You are my pride and joy, a constant source of inspiration and a daily reminder of why I do what I do. When I have a challenging day, all I have to do is look at your photos and it helps me put things into perspective. I love you both so much.

To my wife, Jane: Everything I have accomplished has been made possible because of your constant encouragement and support. You are the rock of this family. I appreciate all your sacrifices. Thank you for believing in me. You've made my life complete.

To my mother, Olympia: You taught me how to be tough and never give up. You are the catalyst who pushed me to continue reaching for my next accomplishments, especially during tough times.

To my father, Kim: The lessons you taught me while working with you at the family convenience store served as a firm foundation for my leadership abilities. The most important concepts I learned from you are humility and to never judge a book by its cover.

To my first editor, Christine Vick: She worked on early versions of this book while battling late-stage cancer. She was a brave woman. I'm honored to have known and worked with her, and I am thankful for all the effort she put into this project.

To my later editors, Dakota Nyght and Blazej Szpakowicz: Thank you for your efforts with this book. I appreciate the time you've both invested in making my voice come through.

To my publisher, Emerald Lake Books: Tara R. Alemany and Mark Gerber expanded my horizon and supported me in this journey. You enabled me to share my work with the world, and I'm grateful for the opportunity.

To my mentor and coach, Paul Martinelli: Thank you for shining a light on me at the live John Maxwell Team leadership summit in 2013. I have learned what it's like to fight through challenges to achieve a dream. Your "Think Grow Rich" program was an eye-opener for me and has been the fire that has kept me going.

To my mentees: You have graciously allowed me to contribute to your growth while I developed my own leadership skills. Serving as a mentor has been an enriching experience, providing me with invaluable insights and lessons gleaned from your unique perspectives and situations. Each of you has played a significant role in my personal and professional development, and I extend my deepest gratitude for the opportunity to journey alongside you.

About the Author

Will Lukang is a change agent, diversity champion, seasoned C-suite executive, and agile coach who focuses on leadership development executive coaching. His colleagues and clients know him as an intuitive professional, skilled presenter, and mental health advocate who can effectively build high-performing teams and consistently deliver innovative solutions and cost-effective results.

Nurturing talent in other people is Will's number one priority because he believes the true measure of a leader is how well they serve others. The cornerstone of his servant leadership practice is the concept of leading by example, a value instilled in him by his father. He believes we can make a greater impact by acting with others rather than alone because, with the right support, motivation and mission, we can achieve incredible things. Regardless of the position, title or degree we hold, seeking to find and bring out the best in others helps to bring out the best in ourselves.

Will coauthored the book *The Character-Based Leader* in 2012, where he leveraged his leadership experience and advanced education in leadership coaching. He frequently designs and delivers effective training and powerful presentations for corporations and teams of all sizes focused on organizational development and talent management.

In addition to his hands-on work, he earned an MBA from Iona College, a master's degree from Seton Hall University, a master's certificate from George Washington University, and a bachelor's degree from the University of Santo Tomas.

In his spare time, Will hosts a podcast called "IWillAim" and is an avid reader and a lifelong learner. Will lives in New Jersey with his wife of nearly thirty years, Jane, and is a father to two young adult daughters.

If you're interested in having Will speak to your group or organization, you can contact him at emeraldlakebooks.com/lukang.

For more great books, please visit us at
emeraldlakebooks.com